# PEOPLE OF ISLAM
Through the Eyes of Friendship

Karen Ann Sigurdson

Karen Ann Sigurdson

Copyright © 2021 by Karen Ann Sigurdson

All Rights Reserved, worldwide. No part of this publication may be reproduced, stored in, or introduced into a retrieval system, or transmitted in any form or by any means (electronic, mechanical, photocopying, recording, or otherwise) without prior written permission, except in the case of brief quotations embodied in critical articles and reviews.

ISBN Amazon

Cover Design by Gerrit H. Van Dyke.

Cover Photo is an artwork depiction of Middle Eastern Window Shutters created by the author's daughter at age 7.

Back cover photo by Karen Ann Sigurdson.

Edited by Nanci Arvizu.

Karen Ann Sigurdson

eyesoffriendship@gmail.com

# DEDICATION

This book is dedicated to those individuals who are disenfranchised and discriminated against because of their religion, gender, race, age or the way they look.

# CONTENTS

| | |
|---|---|
| Acknowledgements | VII |
| Preface | IX |
| Introduction | XVIII |
| 1. Small Town Girl Meets World | 1 |
| 2. The Kingdom | 23 |
| 3. An Expat's Life | 40 |
| 4. Life of the Bedouin | 48 |
| 5. Life in the Desert | 73 |
| 6. In Transition | 94 |
| 7. The Gulf War | 109 |
| 8. Life After Desert Storm | 136 |
| 9. Turkish Hospitality | 155 |
| 10. Egyptian Holiday | 165 |
| 11. A Homestay in Morocco | 180 |

| | |
|---|---|
| 12. When An Expat Returns Home | 189 |
| 13. Sending Song | 198 |
| Appendix | 200 |
| References | 203 |

# ACKNOWLEDGEMENTS

I had been working on my book for a couple of years, and in 2020 became serious about writing it in earnest and finishing it. There were pages of written work, and I had printed some entries for review, only to find out that I had erased the file. I did have many saved pages, but in general, it was a disorganized mess. Thankfully, I met Nanci Arvizu through another channel completely unrelated to writing, and when I found out she was a writer, I knew my book would become a reality. I am very grateful to Nanci for her mentoring as I brought my stories to life, and for the expert editing she provided when my writing was completed. Without Nanci, my book would not have been published.

I am grateful to my many family and friends, who read portions of my manuscript and encouraged me to continue. I am thankful to my children, Gerrit and Hanneke, for their contribution to the book cover. Hanneke contributed a piece she created as a seven-year-old girl in Arabic Culture class while living in Saudi Arabia. I used a photo of this piece for the front cover of the book. Gerrit did a beautiful job in developing the book cover. I am so grateful they were both able to be a part of this project. My husband Dave allowed for flexibility in my work life, giving me the time and energy to bring my book to fruition, and for that, I am very thankful.

And, lastly, my book would not have even been a thought without the life I had in the Middle East, and the wanderlust and interest in people and cultures that followed. I cannot complete this book without mentioning my ex-husband Murray. Without his interest in exotic travel and his desire to work in the Middle East, I am certain I would have never lived the life I did and have had the experiences I shared in my book. Thank you, Murray.

# PREFACE
## Citizen of the World

I am not a writer; I'm a storyteller. Anybody who knows me, or has spent any amount of time around me, knows that I have a story to tell related to just about any subject. When I was considering taking a Head Nurse position in Saudi Arabia in 1990, the man I was dating at the time said, "You might as well, it's all you talk about." Stories of Saudi Arabia were woven into the events of daily life, and this remains true to this day. Ever since I first stepped off the plane onto Middle Eastern soil that hot summer evening in 1982, I have carried with me the stories of those I came to know so well, and the experiences that influenced the person I have become. This book has been living and breathing inside of me for decades, and I am excited to finally share it with you.

I had the honor and privilege to live and work alongside individuals from all over the world. During Desert Storm, it was said that there were nationals from nearly forty countries in the hospital where I worked. Most of these individuals were citizens of countries I had only read about in books. Over time, I began to consider myself a citizen of the world, viewing what was important to me by how it may affect those I grew to love and respect over the years we spent together. When people share meals and work together, especially during a time of war, it becomes clear that there are many shared values and dreams. I found that the majority of people I met just wanted security for themselves and their families, like me.

I lived in Saudi Arabia over the span of many years. My first experience was in the early eighties when my husband and I were employed in a Military Hospital located near the border of Iraq and Kuwait. It was an altogether different time and life, for the most part, seemed quite simple and uncomplicated. There were various crises around the world, but as an American at home, it was only on TV. The Middle East had more recently been in the news as a result of the Iran Hostage Crisis from 1979-1981, and as I reflect on the timeline of events, I wonder why I wasn't more concerned about moving there. Saudi Arabia wasn't Iran, but it was a close neighbor. Naivety can be blamed for many decisions made that in hindsight seem a little crazy. Oh well. So, In 1990, I decided to return to Saudi Arabia and work in a hospital in Riyadh. It just so happened that I arrived in-country a mere week before Iraq's invasion of Kuwait. I'm here to tell you that life in the Kingdom was quite different after the Gulf War.

Islam is the law of the land in Saudi Arabia, and prior to moving there I had little knowledge of its practice, nor of many who claimed to be Muslim. I do recall an Iranian who spent a year at my High School when I was a Freshman or Sophomore, and I remember him taking his prayer rug from his locker to go pray privately. My most memorable experience was my roommate's coworker's marriage to an Iranian gentleman in 1978. We were invited to their wedding, and it was much different than I was accustomed to, mostly due to the absence of alcohol. However, I attended a Southern Baptist wedding shortly after that, and there was no alcohol served either, so similar, but different. Many months after my friend's marriage to her

Iranian husband, she shared stories that highlighted how very different our cultures and religions were. The man truly was the head of the household, which seemed a departure from the norm in a world where women were becoming more independent. I say "seemed" because all these many years later, women are still working for equality in the United States, and the world over. It was helpful to have these basic experiences to reflect on before I arrived in Saudi Arabia in 1982, providing a foundation to build upon.

My first encounter with people of Islam was as a nurse in a military city under construction near the small town of Hafar Al Batin, in the northeastern corner of Saudi Arabia. Those of us working there wondered why the Saudi Arabian Government was spending all this money on a Military Base that would most likely never be used. Eventually, however, the base was very important and instrumental during Operation Desert Shield / Desert Storm Gulf War. Although Saudi Arabia was very peaceful at the time, and the site was actually in a pretty strategic spot if a war broke out in the region.

So many acts of terror at the hands of extremist Muslims have occurred since I returned home from Saudi Arabia in 1994. Unfortunately, since 9/11, many, if not all, Muslims are seen as untrustworthy, or as possible terrorists. Because of this, I became determined to tell my stories of the good people of the Islamic faith I knew, and who treated myself and my family so well. My hope is that in reading these encounters and examples of goodness, that although evil is often at work, the reader might experience what I feel, that the majority of Muslims are good people.

The stories I share are of friends I made when living and traveling in Saudi Arabia and other parts of the world. The people of Islam I knew while working in the Middle East were primarily Saudi Nationals, mainly Bedouin. However, many of my friendships were with people from Egypt, Jordan, Iraq, Lebanon, the United States, Pakistan, and Turkey. It isn't really important where a person is from, or even that they are Muslim. However, for this book, it is important that "I convey an understanding that those I grew to know over the years seemed to share the same hopes and dreams as I had." So, in the end, my friends, whether Islamic or any other religion or background, wanted the same thing I did out of life, to be happy and prosper.

I had experienced various cultural living situations by the time I arrived in Saudi Arabia in 1982. As a result, I had grown accustomed to working alongside others, accepting our differences, with the realization that we were working together to achieve the best outcomes for our patients. Being a nurse is a vocation, not a job. One is called to care for others, and I felt this calling required me to accept my patients and my coworkers as they were and where they were at. My first Saudi assignment took me to a remote desert community, where my patients were primarily Bedouin who lived in the Desert just outside our compound. I learned so much from the women and children who were admitted to our ward for care. It was an experience I have yet to forget almost 40 years later.

In reflection of my time living in the Middle East, I have come to think I was there as an unofficial ambassador of my country. An ambassador of Good Will conveyed through tolerance, friendship, and understanding. This type of ambassadorship is born out of the willingness to leave the comforts of home and the familiar, to venture into the unknown and adhere to the customs of your host country and engage with the locals. This is a familiar concept incorporated in the work of organizations like the Peace Corps, People to People, and many other exchange programs, and I dig it!

I was fortunate to have experiences in the homes of my patients and coworkers and work side by side with my Muslim counterparts while living in the Middle East. When we lived in Hafar Al Batin, I went to work, and was bathed in the culture and the life of the Bedouin. We were invited to their camps and dined in their tents. Life was normal, in a very not normal way. I experienced Prayer Call daily while working in the hospital, and that was "normal."

During my time in Riyadh, my kids and I visited my friend Fatma and her family in Turkey. I had worked with Fatma when working at the King Khalid Military City Hospital in the eighties. She and her husband welcomed my kids and I like we were family. After arriving at her home in Kusadasi, Fatma revealed that she had received notice that an opening had become available for her to be scheduled for a much-needed surgery. In her stead, her husband and niece played host and hostess for several days, and we thoroughly enjoyed and were grateful for their hospitality.

I had a similar experience while visiting Egypt the following year, being treated very hospitably by people who did not even know me prior my meeting them at a medical conference in Cairo. I became friends with a physician from Alexandria, Egypt, and was invited to spend the afternoon at her condo before a Nile Dinner Cruise later that evening. Instead of taking a nap, I stomped through the bowels of Cairo with her twenty-something daughter, and had a blast. My experiences revealed to me that there are friendly people everywhere, and the Middle East was no different.

When I left Saudi Arabia for home almost thirty years ago, I was certain I would return after my kids were grown and on their own. Well, my life took a different path than I had imagined, and it wasn't to be. However, I was able to visit my daughter in 2009, while she was living in Morocco as a Peace Corps volunteer. Morocco's culture is slightly different, but Arabic was spoken, many of the citizens were Muslim, and customs were similar. It was fun to hear her tell stories of Ramadan and attending a Muslim wedding.

Many of the experiences she shared while living in Morocco, I could identify with, and this provided me a sense of comfort during those many months she was away from home.

For the most part, I make it a point to make everyone I meet feel accepted, if only with a smile when encountered. You never know when someone is new and is wanting to feel accepted. In my nursing role, if I find out a patient is originally from an Arabic-speaking country, I make it a point to greet them with a friendly, "Salam Alakum!" Which is "Hello" or "Peace be to you!" in Arabic. The greeting is always well received, usually with a big smile of appreciation that does my heart good!

# INTRODUCTION
## PEOPLE OF ISLAM: THROUGH THE EYES OF FRIENDSHIP

The Call to Prayer sounded in the lobby as I entered through the doors of the hospital one last time. It was July of 1994, and I was going home. I had been a Head Nurse in Pediatrics at the King Fahd Medical City Hospital for the past four years, and it had been like a home to me. As I waited in the beautiful lobby, I took in the sights and aromas I had grown to love. Frankincense and Sandalwood were familiar fragrances I experienced whenever I was out and about in the shops and hotels in Riyadh. Little did I know, as I waited for my taxi that day, that I might never return to Saudi Arabia. I knew it was time for me to go home and develop a life for my kids and I. But, in the back of my mind, I was certain I would return again someday.

I was waiting for my friend Abdulaziz to arrive. I had told him I needed to leave the hospital between three and four that afternoon to catch my plane on time. He asked me to wait until he arrived so that he could say goodbye to me in person. Abdulaziz was my ward's Unit Clerk for a good portion of my four years as Head Nurse. He was not the most reliable when it came to timing, as he was often late to work and was sometimes a no-show. But, I knew Abdulaziz as a kind, caring, genuine human being, and for some reason, because of that, I was willing to give him the benefit of the doubt. I did, however, think he was very good at his job.

While I waited, many of my coworkers, acquaintances, and friends passed by to wish me a fond farewell one last time. There had been party after party for the past month, and although I was going to miss everyone and my work tremendously, I was so tired, I felt I needed to leave just to recuperate. I had already said my goodbyes, but waiting for Abdulaziz gave me the opportunity to enjoy a final gaze across the lobby. This world was in such sharp contrast to my life in the United States. Women were generally covered from head to toe in black abayas, headscarves, and face coverings. The men wore white thobes and gutras or head coverings. I had grown so accustomed to being engulfed in this sea of humanity dressed in black and white. I would miss it.

I became more and more anxious by the minute, wondering if Abdulaziz would arrive on time, and thankfully, he did. "Kareen!" Abdulaziz called out to me, "I have something for you. Thank you for waiting!" And, with a big smile on his face, he approached me, giving me a small carrying case. Inside the case was the most beautiful set of 24-carat gold-rimmed crystal glasses. To this day I'm not sure how I managed to pack the box into my luggage, but you can be certain I did. And, those glasses are a prized possession to this day, a fixture at the table on all special occasions at our house.

I felt like a celebrity that day in the King Fahd Hospital lobby. People who knew me well knew that I was leaving Riyadh, and would not be returning to work. I encountered so many of my coworkers, patients and their families, and colleagues from all branches of the medical field. It seemed like I knew just about everyone who walked by that day. Leaving Saudi Arabia was so bittersweet. My friendships and work accomplishments while living and working in the Kingdom were many, and a piece of me would remain there forever. Although I loved my work and my life in Riyadh, I was moving back to the States to be closer to family and make a life for my kids and I. Once children entered the ninth grade they were no longer able to attend school in Saudi Arabia, so boarding school was the option chosen by most parents. We just took action sooner than later.

I loved my job, my patients, their customs and culture, and the demonstration of a devotion to God that I witnessed daily. As I will express over and over in this book, what I witnessed changed my life; I think for the better. I am by no means an expert on the Islamic religion, nor is the purpose of this book to educate the reader about Islam. The reason for a reference to religion in relating the stories of my life in the Middle East, and the many friendships I formed, is because I would love for others to experience what I did, if only through this book. I knew nothing of the Middle East, and those who lived there, prior to 1982. I'm certain that if I had never lived and worked there, I may either know nothing about it, or only what I learned through news stories and others' experiences. I had a positive experience while living in the Middle East. Perhaps, in my sharing these experiences, it may soften the harshness many feel towards those of the Islamic religion because of the horrors since 9/11 at the hands of monsters claiming their actions in the name of Islam.

Since that terrible day in September of 2001, all too often individuals having Arabic features or displaying their Islamic faith are automatically judged as evil or being dangerous. Witnessing this personally in my daily life, as well as seeing the reporting of crimes against those appearing Muslim, has caused me great sorrow. So, although I had wanted to write about my time in Saudi Arabia prior to 2001, it became most important that I share stories of the people I encountered in my everyday life, at work, in my private life, during my travels and at home. The individuals I speak of, and whose stories I will share, treated me with kindness, dignity, and genuine friendship

I learned about the Islamic religion by witnessing the daily practice and devotion of my coworkers, patients, and friends while living and traveling in the Middle East. I had to look up many of the definitions because it was not something we talked about. It seemed that black in the 80s, we didn't discuss salary, religion, and yes, sex. Today, there are no boundaries where those topics are concerned. So I looked up the definitions I will share with you.

You may well know that Muslims are individuals who believe in and live by the teachings of Islam. There are over two billion people worldwide who call themselves Muslim, making Muslims the world's second-largest group of religious followers. There are two main denominations of Islam, the Sunni Muslims, which total 1.5 billion followers, and 240-340 million Shia Muslims. There are also smaller denominations.

Over the years, we have all heard of people acting out in response to what they believe is asked of them in reverence to Allah, the God of Islam. My understanding, gleaned from research and speaking with learned clergy, is that the Koran does not invite violence nor does it support killing in the name of Allah. I never heard violent words spoken by the individuals I knew or came across while living or traveling in the Middle East or the United States. It was important for me to have a basic understanding of the Islamic religion. Islam was not only the religion, but the law of the land in Saudi Arabia, so I felt it was important to know the rules. I learned much of what I needed to know by observing of those who practiced their religion daily.

In 1992, I was attending a Pediatric Cardiology Conference in Cairo, Egypt. I happened to make friends with a Cardiologist who was all to eager to introduce me to her city and religious practice. She shared with me that she was from Cairo, and proceeded to inform me about the practice of Islam in Egypt, and what was expected of women in Cairo. She said that in Egypt every person was free to practice their religion in the manner they felt called. Dressed in a dark brown long skirt, long-sleeved blouse, and similar colored head cover, she resembled a nun in a traditional habit. It seemed most important to her that I understood an Egyptian Muslim woman could wear the attire she chose. The majority of the Egyptian doctors at the conference wore knee-length skirts and silk blouses, much in contrast to her dress. As our conversation came to a close, my new friend emphasized that that she did not judge a woman by her attire, and that she respected individualism in the practice of religion. What a enlightening exchange I had that day. Actually, I didn't really talk much, I just listened.

Hundreds of thousands of Americans and Expatriates from other countries have lived and worked, and continue to inhabit many of the countries in the Middle East. I was but one person in a sea of foreigners living and working in Saudi Arabia in the eighties and nineties. My story is my own, and many I'm sure had quite different experiences than I. As a nurse working on a Women and Children's Ward, I'm certain I had a much different experience than a man working in telecommunications or construction. I was fortunate to work with women and children, and experience the world they lived in through the stories they shared while in my care. These experiences were often much different than what you might read in a magazine or newspaper, or what you may see on TV.

I have no desire to make a political or moral statement, I'm just not equipped to do so. In a time when intolerance of those with differing viewpoints, nationalities, and religions continues to grow stronger on a seemingly daily basis, it strikes me that sharing positive experiences of living in harmony may be helpful in some way. Please join me as I revisit my journey from small-town girl to world traveler, as I discovered that most people, no matter where they are from, have more similarities than differences. I feel privileged to share the stories of my immersion in the country, the culture, and the religion as portrayed through the lives lived, and acts of kindness and friendship that have never been forgotten.

CHAPTER ONE
## SMALL TOWN GIRL MEETS WORLD
THE JOURNEY BEGINS

Did you ever wonder why things happen the way they do in life, whether the goals or intentions of your youth have an effect on who you marry, where you live, and what type of work you do? Well, to be honest, I never really thought about my life in this way. But, looking back over the years, I recall a moment in time that may have shaped my future. I was about ten years old and, for some reason, contemplating my future. This occurrence is truly the only time I remember contemplating what I wanted to do or be when I grew up. I was sitting on the floor, looking over a collection of books housed in a bookcase in the hallway next to my bedroom. I don't have a memory the book's title, but I remember declaring that I wanted to be a missionary when I grew up. I truly believe that in making that declaration I set in motion the trajectory of my life.

Years later my mother shared with me that she wanted to be a missionary when she was growing up, but it never happened. I thought that was weird. But, you often hear of children fulfilling dreams their parents had, without ever knowing it was a desire of theirs. My mother went on to become a nurse, which is a very similar calling, especially in the way she served her community.

My childhood was pretty average, to say the least. I doubt I would have been voted the one most likely to live and work halfway around the world by my graduating class. But, incredibly, that is my story. I lived in and traveled to countries I don't even remember studying in school. It's amazing to me how life evolved in an almost effortless manner; but perhaps, that's the magic of intention with the added benefit of youth. This is how it all began.....

I enjoyed a fairly uncomplicated life, growing up in the sixties in Small Town USA. My family lived on a rather quiet street not far from downtown, and because there were a lot of kids in the neighborhood, it wasn't necessary to venture too far from home to have someone to "play" with. My mother worked outside the home while I was young, but there were plenty of stay-at-moms to keep an eye on our activities. We kids generally got along pretty well, and if we didn't, we generally figured things out without having to involve our parents. A fight between older boys broke out from time to time, but usually nothing serious. If things got out of hand, parental involvement was invited. So, if we watched ourselves and how we went about things, we could pretty much do as we wished. I mention this to provide a backdrop for how I approached life later on.

As you might imagine, even in the sixties, there were those who were bullies and those who were made fun of or bullied. I didn't really understand all that, but I was a subject of such activity at one point, and it was awful. Unfortunately, one doesn't always know the damage being done when making fun of others, especially when you're young, and it's not you. But, many years after graduating high school, several of my classmates and I were made aware of the damage done because of the inability to accept another's differences. I found it painful to think that

I may have been a part of it, if even in a small way. Not taking action is often as bad as causing the actual harm. Who knows, these experiences may have helped to shape who I became, and how I look at the world and its inhabitants. Having experience with hurt and seeing others hurt can soften or harden an individual, you never know. Ultimately, I think it caused me to develop compassion for the underdog or oppressed.

 I loved my hometown and had planned to return to live there when I finished college. I honestly never felt a need to move away and be a part of the world at large. I loved the security of knowing where everything was, how things were done, and having friends I knew my whole life. But, when I reflect back, I can see how it evolved in a way that would never allow this to be. Looking back, I can recall a time when I was about 10 years old and, for some reason, contemplating my future. Perhaps, life wasn't so idyllic after all, and I was already thinking of getting away. This occurrence is truly the only time I remember thinking about what I wanted to do or be when I grew up. I was sitting upstairs in my parent's house, looking over a collection of books housed in a bookcase, in the hallway next to my bedroom. I don't have a memory of the book I was looking at, but I remember declaring to my Great Aunt Anne that I wanted to be a missionary when I grew up. This event never crossed my mind when I was planning and eventually accepted a position in the medical mission field in 1981. However, I now believe that in my making that declaration, the trajectory for my life's journey was set in motion. I know today that having a dream or intention, and declaring it, is an important step in making that dream come true, even if you don't know that's what you're doing.

My Background

As I said, my mother was a nurse. She grew up in a Wisconsin farming community, the daughter of Norwegian immigrants. While in Nursing School, she left home to train at Cook County Hospital in Chicago in the late 40s. I can assure you that working at Cook County Hospital even then was an eye-opening experience as far as a lesson in diversity. I imagine this experience was instrumental in making her the compassionate, giving person she became. She later went on to work at the VA Hospital in Madison,

Wisconsin where she met my father. He was actually a patient of hers, undergoing follow-up treatment for TB he had acquired while serving in the South Pacific. Now, that's a story in itself. "A small-town Wisconsin girl meets and marries an Army Veteran, originally from Chicago, recovering from TB on the ward where she is working as a nurse." While I was growing up, my mother was the Nursing Supervisor of our County's Public Health Nursing Program. She was often called in the middle of the night to address an urgent issue, and would not hesitate to go out if needed. I can honestly say that I never heard her complain about this. She always spoke of her job and the people she cared for in a responsible, compassionate manner. I don't ever recall her speaking of her patients or their circumstances in a judgmental way. My mother often shared a time when she was about 5 years old, and some girls accompanied her home from school one day. All these many years later, she still recalls them telling her parents that they couldn't play with her anymore because they can't understand her. She didn't speak English. My grandparents sent her to school to learn English. I guess they didn't know it would be a problem. Well, my mother learned English, and her younger brother never learned how to speak Norwegian. I'll never know, but I would venture to say that this incident caused my mother to be the more inclusive and less judgmental person I witnessed growing up.

The son of an Icelandic immigrant, my father was born in North Dakota and spent much of his formative years as a young man in Chicago. Sometime after immigrating to the United States, my grandfather met my grandmother in North Dakota, while he was working as a Superintendent of schools and as a clerk in a small shoe store. My grandmother was actually from Wisconsin. So you see, my family has always been on the move. The family soon relocated to Chicago when my grandfather accepted a transfer with the Immigration Service. The family wintered on the Texas/Mexico border near Brownsville, Texas for my grandfather's work. So, it's safe to say that my father grew up with a variety of life experiences unlike most youngsters during the Depression. When World War II broke out, my father enlisted and was stationed in the South Pacific. Over the years I listened to the stories he shared about his many experiences, and what it was like to grow up in Chicago. The stories filled me with wonder for the possibilities the future might hold.

And, then there was my Aunt Anne. She was actually my father's aunt and my great aunt, and one of the biggest influences of my young life. My Aunt Anne was a rock. She was unmarried, and because of that, she was the one in the family called upon to come to the rescue whenever there was a need. When I was young, she told me of the time she left her job and love interest in Milwaukee when the family needed her to return home to care for her mother, who had suffered a stroke. After her mother died, she moved to Chicago to be a "nanny" to my father and uncle while they were growing up, and when my grandparents retired to a lake home in Wisconsin, my Aunt Anne joined them. After they passed away, she continued to live in the country without running water, electricity, or a telephone. The house was wired, so she would use a generator occasionally to vacuum the carpets. My Aunt Anne was a truly remarkable person. I don't really think she was afraid of anything. I spent a great deal of time with her "out at the lake," and learned something about self-sufficiency. She lived to be 96 years old, still spending summers on the lake well into her nineties. Her example and the lessons I learned just watching her live life gave me the courage to be fearless and not always have all the answers before I ventured into the unknown.

The world I grew up in was one of endless possibilities, where anyone could do anything, and all people were equal, so I thought. I am grateful for that perspective. It's quite amazing that the assassination of President Kennedy did not leave a dark shadow on the future I envisioned, but I guess that's the beauty of youth. Like many of my generation, I remember hearing President Kennedy's inaugural speech, asking us to consider, "Not what your country can do for you, but what you can do for your country," and I listened to the "I Have a Dream" speech and was inspired by it. When Martin Luther King, Jr. and Bobby Kennedy were killed, my naïveté told me it was merely the acts of evil men, and I continued to have confidence that the future was bright. Even if I didn't actually intellectualize that way of thinking, I do think I believed it at my very core.

Rochester, Minnesota

I moved away from home at the age of eighteen to go to college. Little did I know, except for school breaks and summer vacation, I would never return to live in my hometown again. Actually, I would live outside of Wisconsin for most of my adult life. In college, I was exposed to people from all over the world and introduced to different religions, cultures, and races. For some reason, I was always very interested in finding out about where a person was from, and how their background compared to mine, what if any experiences we shared. Race and religion never seemed to matter, because there was so much more to talk about. I spent my first year in Wisconsin and then was fortunate to transfer to a school where I would complete my nurse's training in Rochester, Minnesota. While training at the Mayo clinic affiliated hospitals, I not only cared for patients from other countries and cultures but also worked with individuals who came to Rochester to work or study at the famous Mayo Clinic. It seemed natural to walk the halls and work alongside others, as a citizen of the world.

Side note: Upon reflection, I have often wondered if my college transfer was a time when my desire to be a missionary all those years before impacted the course of my life. I was not accepted into the nursing program after my Freshman year, and I was pretty devastated. However, in retrospect, my training at the hospitals affiliated with the Mayo Clinic turned out to be quite a feather in my cap. To this day, people are impressed if I tell them where I trained. And, I have to say, I received a great education and met my friend whom I moved to Galveston, Texas with to start our nursing careers.. Interesting!

Galveston, Texas

My roommate and I moved to Galveston, Texas to work at the University of Texas Medical Branch right after graduation. My training and hospital work while at the Mayo Clinic affiliated hospitals provided me an education in diversity that enabled me to transition to a life in Galveston, Texas fairly easily. I had come to realize that most people share more similarities than differences. I began work as a staff nurse in the Child Health Center on the UTMB campus in Galveston. Many of my coworkers who were native to Texas honestly thought that I was from a Scandinavian country, and was new to the United States.

It seems that many of the older nurse's assistants that I worked with hadn't known anyone from Wisconsin, so really had no reason to know where it was on the map. And because I was so fair-skinned and blonde, they seemed to think that I was from Scandinavia. Actually, it was as good a guess as any given until this time, there were perhaps few workers from North Central Wisconsin. Because of a nursing shortage at that time, nurses were being recruited from all over the States and Canada. It was an eye-opening experience being a minority. The experience served me well in the years to come.

Living in Texas was like being in another country; the pace was so much slower than what I was used to, and the spoken English was very different. I couldn't understand the dialect of many people I worked with for the first several months. Although Texas is obviously a part of the United States, and the folks I worked with were Americans, living in Texas was quite the culture shock. For at least six months, I could barely understand any of what my coworkers were saying, and it was important that I did understand. We were caring for children as a team, so communication was key. We often spent time talking with patients and their parents in a more casual manner. During these times, if the conversation was not a serious one, I figured I didn't need to understand every word spoken. I became weary of always having to say "excuse me" or "pardon me" several times throughout the conversation. So, if I didn't understand something that was said, and I missed a word or two, I would laugh if they laughed or I would nod in agreement if that seemed appropriate. However, the day did finally arrive when I understood most of what was being said. That was a wonderful day of accomplishment.

Happily, in the time it took for me to fully participate in a conversation, somehow I had become accepted as part of the "team." It seemed that as a result of my persistence, my coworkers came to believe that I cared about what they had to say and that I was interested in them as individuals. I did care about them and valued their commitment to the work we did. It was my first lesson in how important it is to engage with people where they're at, and the simple act of learning the language of those you work with is a huge part of being a team.

I met my first husband Murray while working as a nurse at UTMB. Murray was a resident, arriving on the scene after I had been working on the Pediatric Ward for a year. He had just started his internship, and Pediatrics was his first rotation. Murray had a dry sense of humor and was a gifted doctor. I was quite taken with him, and obviously, he was smitten with me. Having traveled extensively in Europe prior to medical school, he had some world experiences I found very appealing. At some point, we talked of marriage, and about our life plans after his residency was completed. I vividly recall a scene where we were deep in conversation about work as medical missionaries after Galveston. Most, if not all, of our friends in the Residency program were going on to good-paying jobs and a mortgage. Not us! We were off to sites unknown. I still find it incredible that Murray was open to volunteer work as husband and wife, doctor and nurse. The financial compensation would be small, but the reward great. I believe this is yet another example of the course my life took as a result of the stated intention made when I was ten years old. Yeah, unbelievable is the word!

Murray completed his Family Medicine Residency in June of 1981. Originally from Canada, he had been in the United States for three years on a Visa granted for Medical Residency training. We had married the year before and were working with an Immigration Lawyer to facilitate Murray's Green Card application, so we could move forward with our plans after Residency. We were planning to take a Spanish Immersion Course in Cuernavaca, Mexico that summer to better equip us as volunteers in South America. We had been working with Catholic Relief Services and had passed all their screening requirements. Everything was completed, and we were waiting for our assignment. However, right after Murray completed his residency, our lawyer informed us that it was determined that he would have to return to Canada. Well, that was not happening! The next day we were able to go to the Immigration Office in Houston, we went. Murray and I stood in line with many others seeking a Visa or Green Card allowing them to remain in the country. That morning we walked into the building that housed the US Immigration Office, uncertain of the outcome, but later that day, we walked out with Murray's temporary Green

Card. He was told that he had to remain in the country until he received his permanent Green Card, which was projected to be at least two months.

St. Lucia, The West Indies

Unfortunately, but not unexpectedly, our plan for the summer Immersion course in Mexico was scrapped. But, that was a small price to pay, in light of what could have transpired. It just so happened that in the summer of 1981, Catholic Nuns and Priests were being killed at the hands of what were thought to be drug lords and their followers. We would not be going to South America after all, and now we had time to make another plan. We eventually received an assignment through the Direct Relief Foundation to work as medical missionaries in St. Jude Hospital on the southern tip of the small island nation of Saint Lucia. By November of 1981, we were off to St. Lucia, and in for a change in hospital culture according to the British Medical system. There was a whole different set of rules of conduct in the community also, but that was okay. I truly believe, when in Rome, do as the Romans do. I believe when you visit a foreign country, it's important to respect the customs and mores of the home country. By the time we arrived in Saudi Arabia, I was ready for just about anything. For some reason, I have always been pretty adaptable. This trait would come in handy in our new desert home.

Sometime in February or March of 1982, a New York Times Newspaper arrived on an airplane from the States. New arrivals routinely brought American newspapers and magazines for the volunteers who had been on the island for some time and missed reading the latest news and gossip often overlooked when reported by the BBC or a Caribbean radio station or newspaper. Hidden deep within the bowels of the New York Times was an ad recruiting Physicians for a hospital somewhere in Saudi Arabia. Little did I know that Murray was the least bit interested in working in Saudi Arabia. I guess he had had his fill of working as a Hospitalist, which included being on call, for room and board and a $100 monthly stipend. He never once complained about our volunteer commitment, but when he saw this job opportunity as a real possibility, it was all over. We didn't really talk about it much, but the wheels were set in motion once Murray called the number in the ad. Before we knew it, we were on our way to Georgia for an interview and returned with two job offers in hand. Murray was offered a position in one of the clinics, and it just so happened that the hospital was about to open a women and Children's wing, and desperately needed a Head Nurse with Pediatric experience. Bingo!

Hafar Al Batin, Saudi Arabia

It was very hard to leave St. Lucia and the friends we had made. We had originally committed to a one-year contract at St. Jude Hospital. The administrator at the time was very gracious in accepting our resignation. St. Lucia had been our home for the past 5 months, and it was difficult to say goodbye to the hospital, the beaches, and most of all the kind people of the small Island nation. We left St. Lucia just after Easter that year. We required work visas to enter Saudi Arabia, so it was a waiting game for the next several weeks. We spent several days in New York City until I received my Visa, and then almost a month in Toronto waiting for Murray's Visa. Neither one of us knew anything about Saudi Arabia, so we spent hours in libraries and bookstores looking for relevant material on the subject.

Remember, there was no Internet back then. It just so happened that the book The Kingdom had just been released in bookstores. We immediately bought the book, and devoured it, reading it from cover to cover in a couple of days. We read the words, but it was very hard to relate to life in The Kingdom. That was okay. At least we had a reference point from which to begin our journey.

I moved to Saudi Arabia in 1982 for a job, and because my husband wanted to. It was that simple. I probably would never have moved to Saudi Arabia if it wasn't for Murray's urging, and, for that, I am very grateful. I had just turned twenty-seven prior to leaving the United States for the Middle East. But, by this point in my life, I had moved several times for school and work, and I was quite accustomed to change. Relocating wasn't hard for me; I saw it as an adventure. As a nurse, I was naturally interested in people, and I loved to learn about people and their customs, as well as where they were from. The ultimate destiny really didn't matter to me, as the whole world was basically an unknown. If it was something new, I wanted to learn about it. During my brief stint in St. Lucia, I started taking French Patois classes to learn the local dialect. I wanted to be able to understand my patients and speak to them in their native tongue while caring for them.

Moving to Saudi Arabia meant learning Arabic if I wanted to converse with my patients. So, I had to start all over learning another language. You can't read Arabic like you do French or Spanish, so I had to learn the language by listening and repeating words and phrases. Over time, I managed to learn words used most often in the hospital setting. It provided a good foundation. Except for what we gleaned from reading The Kingdom, my husband and I knew little about what to expect of everyday life in Saudi Arabia, the culture or the religion. But, we were eager to dive in and get started, and that is what we did.

I soon realized that the majority of my patients were Bedouin, nomads who lived in encampments in the surrounding desert outside the compound. Life in the desert was hard to envision; I imagined it as a lifelong camping trip, but much harder. I was Head Nurse of a Women and Children's Ward and took care of women and children from birth to death. During the two years of my assignment in this region of Saudi Arabia, I became intimately acquainted with the Bedouin culture, the Arabic language, and the Muslim religion, through the daily encounters I experienced with my patients and coworkers. We were all on a journey together. Thank goodness the nurses working on my ward had been in the country for some time before I arrived and were familiar with the language and the culture.

Most of the nurses working on my ward were from the Philippines and spoke pretty good Arabic. There was also a nurse from Turkey, whose native tongue was Arabic, and then a couple of the nurses were from Thailand, who were fairly proficient in Arabic. Thankfully, we also had an Arabic Interpreter. These individuals were my mentors as I maneuvered my new job and the environment I found myself in. Acclimating to my new country was going to take time. This was an adventure of a lifetime, and I had no idea what to expect from one moment to the next. Thank goodness I had a strong nursing foundation, working as a staff nurse and Head Nurse in Galveston and as a volunteer nurse in the West Indies. Let's go back to that first day, because it really was pretty special, beginning with our landing at the Dhahran International Airport on one very hot summer day as the sun was setting in the

West. Please allow me to introduce you to the special people and everyday events of life that were anything but ordinary.

Chapter Two
# THE KINGDOM
Arrival and Immersion

It was the summer of 1982, and the plane we boarded in New York City many hours earlier had just landed at the Dhahran International Airport. The sun looked like a ball of fire in the sky, as it made its descent over the horizon, and then disappeared into the Persian Gulf. This time in my life was all so surreal. Little did I know that as I stepped off the plane that evening, I was entering a chapter that would forever define my future. At the time in history when we arrived in the Kingdom, Saudi Arabia was a very peaceful place, and I found living there very secure and full of adventure at the same time. Little did we know that this region would eventually experience insecurity, as a result of war and dissent in the years to come.

Thankfully, we were able to experience the calm before the storm.

We were engulfed in a sea of white and black. The men wore white thobes, essentially a long shirt, coupled with the traditional white and red headcover. Women were adorned head to toe in a black abaya and scarf. The abaya was a light cover worn over a long dress, and women wore scarves on their heads and covered their faces in black, with only their eyes visible. It was quite an unusual initiation, black and white figures scurrying about in all directions. As I said, there was no internet in those days, so there was no way to prepare for what we would encounter on our arrival. I remember wondering whether the servers in the restaurant were Saudi Nationals but soon realized that most of the service workers were from other countries, such as Bangladesh, Sri Lanka, India, and Pakistan. Hospital workers often originated from the Philippines. It was a bit confusing at first, to say the least, but it all made sense before long.

It seemed that for many of the Saudi Arabian citizens, education of any kind was still limited and advanced education out of reach, except for the rich or offspring of the already educated. So, when we arrived in 1982, many if not all of the service positions were filled by international workers. Personnel was also recruited internationally to manage hospitals and provide patient care in the hospitals that had just been built or were in the process of being built. Corporations with expertise in every specialty of engineering and construction were contracted to work in all parts of Saudi Arabia, as well. It was the Expat's world, and the sky was the limit as far as jobs to be had if you were willing to travel and leave your country.

Once through Immigration, we were met by a member of Whittaker International's Human Resources team. As a representative of the hospital we would be working for, this individual was stationed in Dhahran to meet new arrivals, and assist them in undergoing the necessary screening, as well as all that was needed for a hospital I.D. and in-country travel. These are tasks usually performed within the hospital on the first day of orientation, but we soon found that working and living in Saudi Arabia was very different from the requirements needed to live and work in the States and recently in the West Indies. Thankfully, the main priority for our first night in Country was to settle comfortably into our room, make it to the dining room before it closed, and to hopefully sleep. We stayed at a lovely hotel, the room was beautiful and the meals were wonderful. I felt like I was walking around in a dream. We were basically picked up and brought to this hotel and told to eat and drink whatever we fancied, and then a transport would be waiting for us after breakfast the next morning to take us into town to complete the necessary paperwork. We were like two college freshmen arriving on campus with our belongings, having no idea of what to expect, but filled with the nervous expectations that accompany the unknown.

Murray and I absolutely collapsed from fatigue that night, we were so exhausted. We left Toronto the morning we were scheduled to fly to Saudi Arabia, waited in the JFK Airport in New York pretty much all day, and then boarded the plane for Dhahran later that night. We were extremely lucky to fly first class, for neither of us had ever flown 13 hours non-stop to anywhere before. So, when we finally made it to our final destination, we were ready for a good night's sleep, to say the least! The next morning, after breakfast, we joined the group of new arrivals and boarded a hospital van, and were taken to a clinic for physical exams and photos required for our work permits. When that was completed, we were off to an open market to shop for items to help make our new living quarters more like home.

The open-air market we shopped at was an experience all its own. In the States, when you go to an outdoor mall or indoor mall, there are usually a few department stores, and an abundance of specialty shops selling different types of commodities, not a whole lot of repetition. In Saudi Arabia, when I was there in the eighties and nineties, you would find many stores right next to each other selling the same commodities. There might be 6 stores selling hardware, and then several selling lamps, and so on. So, shopping involved a good deal of walking if you needed various items sold in different stores. I found it a bit strange. Well, that day, we didn't really need much, because we didn't even know what our living quarters would be like. We did know, however, that we needed something to play our music on, and we needed a radio. So, our newest prized possession was a JVC Boom Box.

Murray had made several cassettes of our favorite music prior to leaving the States, and we added an extensive collection of music while living in the Caribbean. To us, the Boom Box was a necessity. Listening to the radio while living in St. Lucia became our lifeline to the outside world because we would go days without a current newspaper, and we didn't have a TV. Life in Saudi Arabia, where we would be living, was much the same in regards to having ready access to current news and the lack of a TV signal. So, you see, our BoomBox was for much more than playing music or enjoyment. That was for sure! We also bought a few odds and ends to brighten up our place. Shopping in Saudi Arabia is a favorite pastime of many ExPats, but having just arrived, we didn't have the cash to enjoy it.

The Holy Month of Ramadan was about to begin in a few days, and luckily our Human Resources contact explained exactly what Ramadan was and how it might affect us. Usually, if there is a religious holiday, those observing the holiday participate however is their custom, and those unaffected go about their lives. Not so in Saudi Arabia, especially during Ramadan. During Ramadan, there is a period of fasting throughout the day from sun-up to sundown. No one is to eat in public during Ramadan, whether Muslim or not. And, in observance, all individuals are encouraged to conduct themselves in a very conservative manner, especially where women's dress is concerned. So, I bought a couple of caftans, thinking they were quite conservative and would be acceptable articles of clothing for a young woman. That completed our shopping for the day. Not too terribly exciting, but adequate!

On returning to the hotel, we were informed that there was a good chance we would be staying another night due to the weather. So, we were game for another night of relaxation, even though we were eager to reach our final destination. But, with very little notice the plan changed, and it was decided that a driver would take the band of us across the desert to our new home. We left the hotel sometime around 8 or 9 pm and were off on our first excursion across the barren desert with our newfound friends. I recall it being pretty warm in the van, but because there was no sun, it was tolerable. We left the windows open, and a warm breeze seemed to provide the necessary reprieve from the residual heat of the day. We started off for our "compound" just after dusk; the moon must have been close to full because you could see a fair amount of the desert as we traveled. There were no buildings to be seen, and we encountered few cars after leaving the city limits of Dhahran and Al Khobar.

If you look up barren desert in the dictionary, it describes to a T what the landscape was like as we traveled the highway from Dhahran to our compound near the Iraq/Kuwait border. I didn't know what to expect from one moment to the next. Initially, I wondered whether there would be mountains or trees of some sort. But no, there was little foliage, let alone a tree! There was nothing to look at except sand. But, to be quite honest, I found it to be quite interesting and beautiful. It's amazing how beauty is found in simplicity. The moon had no competition that night, and the night sky was illuminated with a myriad of stars glistening up against the blank canvas that was the desert. I have lived in the desert most of my life now, and that feeling of wonder I experienced that first night has never left me.

Various styles of music filled the van as we drove down the highway into the night. It was kind of like going to summer camp. We were all getting to know each other for the first time, so there was a great deal of conversation and laughter. Murray and I were exhausted, but I couldn't sleep; so I spent hours looking out the window eager to see anything that would help me define the journey. I was trying to adjust to the reality that this country was my new home. The trip was actually a bit boring and uneventful until we came upon a donkey crossing the road, and the van we were traveling in hit it. The driver didn't even hesitate for a moment or stop, he just kept right on going. That was pretty much the excitement of the trip. I was afraid that somehow law enforcement would find out that the driver hit the donkey and didn't stop, and we'd be detained. But that never happened. We continued into the night without further incident.

It was helpful to have had that period of several weeks in New York City and Toronto to kind of buffer or cleanse the palate from living in a tropical paradise on the island of St. Lucia. Even though we were volunteers, and lived in marginal housing, the experience was so lovely and magical in its own right. It's incredible how things transpire, but when you are volunteering your time and talents, especially in full-time medical work, people of means love to shower you with fringe benefits, such as outings on a sailboat, or invitations to barbecues and parties. We even attended a Scottish Highland Dance one evening, complete with bagpipes and Scottish delicacies. Memories of our island paradise, and the many friends we made over the months, danced in my head as we traveled across the desert to the unknown.

It was hard to believe that my husband Murray and I had made the decision to leave our work in St. Lucia and move to a King Khalid Medical City Compound in the middle of nowhere. The place was hard to envision even with the assistance of a map, as Hafar Al Batin was a camel trading post, and was not even on the map of Saudi Arabia. How had we allowed ourselves to be talked into this, I wondered! Even today when I tell people that I had worked there in the eighties and nineties, many know little of the country and its people, except for what's been reported in the media. Unfortunately, the evil that has been done at the hands of a collection of Saudi Nationals and members of the Royal Family reflects badly on the whole country.

Luckily, the book "The Kingdom, Arabia and the House of Saud," written by Robert Lacy, had just been released about the time we were preparing to leave the United States for the Middle East. The book documented the struggles and victories of the House of Saud, led by King Saad, the founder of Saudi Arabia. It thoroughly chronicled his reign and provided a history of the Bedouin Rivalries and how they shaped the future of Saudi Arabia, as well as the cultural and economic transition as a result of the discovery of oil. We read the book over and over again, as we immersed ourselves in the culture and customs of The Kingdom. We used it as a reference manual.

By the time we arrived, Saudi Arabia was considered to have entered the "modern" era. The country seemed modern in many ways if you were in Riyadh, Dhahran, or Jeddah, but it is important to note that in 1982, the Arabic Calendar was still in the 1400s. The book prepared us somewhat, in regards to basic customs and important holidays, but living in this new reality was quite a different story. It spoke in depth about the relationships with one to four wives a Saudi man may have, and how a man must conduct himself in relation to providing financial and emotional support equally to all wives. This custom was obviously very new and weird to us, but it was one we grew to accept. In all actuality, unless a man is very rich, it is uncommon for one to have more than two wives. There were other topics covered, and I recall making fun of some I didn't understand. Over time, I realized that acceptance was an easier route, and in spending time with my patients, subjects that seemed very different made sense in their world.

Time slowly passed as we continued down the road, and I used the time to review our recent comings and goings against the backdrop of the desert. At long last, sometime just before four in the morning, we reached the Guard Gate of the Front Entry to the King Khalid Military City compound. We made it! As was protocol, our van was searched for contraband, and our papers were checked. This was something very different and new for us, but over time was a very common occurrence and seemed pretty normal. Next, we were off to the Security Office where we would receive further review and relinquish our Passports.

"What did I just say?" Yes, we had to give the Human Resources/Security Department our passports. My initial response was, "No, we can't give up our passport, we've traveled to other countries and never relinquished our passports. You'll have to go about this a different way, this is just not possible" Well, guess what? We had to turn over our passports and leave the office with a photocopy.

We were eventually taken to our new home and, as we fell asleep, wondered to ourselves what the Hell had just happened. The van that dropped us off only hours before, returned for us around eight o'clock and drove us to the hospital. We obviously didn't get a whole lot of rest, but we were so excited, sleep was near impossible. Upon arrival for our first day of orientation in the hospital, we received a brief Arabic lesson which included the basic greetings necessary to start work and conduct ourselves in a polite manner. As is customary in every language I had been introduced to in past work and travels, knowing how to say "Hello, How are you? Hello," in response, and "I am fine," or something similar is very helpful. Throughout the book, included in stories, I will include some of the basic greetings and short sentences that were necessary to engage in a manner that could be understood. Knowing these basic phrases enabled me to feel a part of, and I believe, helped my patients and their families feel that I was interested in them, and cared enough to learn their language.

I immersed myself in the customs, culture, and language of Saudi Arabia, which is heavily influenced by its Islamic roots. The days passed with regularity, accompanied by prayer calls that occurred with precision. Prayer call was the one thing you could expect on time. I accepted that the way especially the women dressed was a reflection of the reserved countenance deemed acceptable. When we visited Saudi families, women had their own quarters, whether in a tent or villa, and men socialized with men in their own quarters, either a room or a tent. Thanks to the two male Social Workers who met us on that first day, I was able to slowly acclimate to how things were done in the hospital. I was the Head Nurse of my unit, so I expected myself to provide nursing care in a respectful manner related to customs and religious rules, how to address females and males appropriately, and which words or terms in Arabic were the most necessary in the hospital environment.

As I said previously, there were certain greetings and phrases I was taught early on to ease my transition to my position in the hospital. As is anywhere, no matter where you live, certain phrases are used on a daily basis, every day, all day. Many of the Arabic words and phrases I learned during those early days, I continue to use regularly around the house today. I say "Alhumdulalah" when expressing my gratitude to God or "Inshaalah", when asking for life to unfold according to His will. It is just as easy to say in English, but the practice became a habit while living in Saudi Arabia because I heard it used all day, every day when talking with my patients, coworkers, and the public in general. And, to be quite honest, it sounds beautiful.

I had learned Spanish and used it often when caring for patients in Galveston. When we lived in St. Lucia briefly, I started attending French Patois classes so I could speak to patients who did not speak English. But, in Saudi Arabia, it was quite different. The majority, if not all, patients, spoke only Arabic and did not understand a word of English.

Unfortunately, we did not have an interpreter on all the shifts 7 days a week, so the need to use the language was of greater importance. I wanted to provide the care my patients needed and deserved, which meant that I knew enough of their language to understand their needs. I may not have learned Classical Arabic, but my attempt at Arabic allowed me to converse with my patients at a degree that was comfortable for all parties. I could greet my patients, and ask questions regarding their comfort and needs, and I could understand basic responses and when a deeper understanding was needed, it was time to engage an interpreter.

The first phrase I was taught by my hospital mentors was how to politely say hello. "As-salāmu 'alaykum" is an Arabic greeting that means peace be upon you. The greeting is a standard citation among Muslims whether socially or within worship and other contexts. As-Salam Alaykum was the first greeting we learned. The first greeting of the day, no matter what time of day it was.

I loved to engage in conversation with my Arabic coworkers and other hospital workers I encountered daily, as well as my patients and their families. It was fun knowing how to speak a small phrase fundamental to developing a relationship with my patients and those with Arabic roots. Although the official language of the hospital I worked in was English and Arabic, it was expected that English would be spoken by hospital personnel, but out of respect for the country I was employed in, I thought it reasonable to learn Arabic, if I could.

## Chapter Three
# An Expat's Life
### Hafer Al Batin and Riyadh

It's hard to explain what life was like living in Saudi Arabia over thirty years ago to someone who has never been. Although one can search the Internet for information on just about any topic, it's still nearly impossible to truly understand a way of life without being immersed in it. It is even hard for me to relate my life in the States to my life while living in the Middle East. If it's difficult for me to contrast and compare the various aspects of life in the different cultures, I imagine it's near impossible for one who hasn't stepped foot in the country. This is illustrated when someone will ask me questions about my time in Saudi Arabia, and then may share their impression of what they think it must have been like. Quite often what they have read or been led to believe was not my experience. Obviously, I haven't been in Saudi Arabia in over 25 years. But, a physician friend of mine was there recently for a Medical Conference and he told me of his visit. He said that our hospital seemed to be flourishing and his medical colleagues where very welcoming and professional, as he remembered them.

When I set off for my first contract in Saudi Arabia, there was no reference for me to envision what to expect. The same is true when people I knew from other parts of the world shared with me their impression of the average American. Their description was often gleaned from watching TV shows about people living in New York City or one of the main cities in California. Well, I'm from Northern Wisconsin, and there are millions of Americans who live outside of New York and California. I hope you get my point.

Living and working in Saudi Arabia was a perfect way to get to know people from all over the world. The compound we lived on had construction workers from Korea and Pakistan, and hospital personnel hailed from all over the world, including Great Britain, Australia, Various countries in Africa, Turkey, the Philippines, Thailand, and the United

States. The Army Corps of Engineers were housed on a neighboring compound, so The U.S. had a major influence in the area. It seems that people have been leaving their home countries for jobs and volunteer work in other countries for decades before my husband and I moved to the Middle East in 1982. I guess I was pretty naive. I didn't even know what an Expat or Ex-patriot was, and I would venture to guess that many Americans are also unfamiliar with the term. There are Ex-patriots from all over the world, living and working in other countries, some for many years. Many Expatriates leave their families and home countries to work elsewhere and receive better pay and benefits than they might perform similar work at home. I became an Expat without even knowing it. I had heard that an American citizen was able to earn more money outside of the United States without being charged income tax on a large percentage of it, if out of the country for long enough periods of time. And, because of the fact that housing and travel were included in our work contract, my husband and I were able to pump that money back into the American and world economies while on vacation in the various countries we visited. Seems pretty cool! It's a Win-Win situation for all concerned.

My coworkers were my family and friends for the two years I lived on the KKMC compound and worked on the ward in our little support hospital. In many ways, the women who delivered their babies at our hospital, often later accompanying a sick child while hospitalized, were often like family. We celebrated babies being born, as well as birthdays and anniversaries, of patients while hospitalized, just as you would in the United States. The population we served was limited, so many of our patients returned to our unit again and again in various capacities. The compound we lived on was pretty isolated, and I worked 48 hours a week, so there was little time for other activities outside of work. Interaction with our patients was a big part of life on KKMC, and spending time talking and becoming familiar with customs and the language was very important to me. The hours flew by, and although the work was often challenging, it was enjoyable because our work offered services that would otherwise not be available to the population of Bedouin living in the region. We were their lifeline, for the most part, and we learned to depend on each other. We got to know each other well, and it was a fun and interesting experience, learning firsthand how similar and different we were.

Living in a very remote region of Saudi Arabia, and working forty-eight hours a week, afforded us special benefits. It was determined that living and working on the KKMC Compound was a bit of a hardship, so we were given a paid R&R (Rest and Relaxation) leave every three months. The majority of the hospital staff was able to get out on some sort of leave every three to four months. Most of the staff from Western countries took the entire three weeks to go somewhere, and once a year the hospital corporation paid the airfare back to the staff's country of origin and provided an annual Home Leave of thirty days. It was very common to hear folks saying, as the time drew nearer for their leave, "Twenty-four days and a wake-up, and then finally, one day and a wake-up!" We were very eager to go on leave, and with little to spend our earnings on, we could save it for our future or spend a good amount on a nice holiday, as they call it in Britain.

I was in for a rude awakening when I left the United States in regards to how citizens of other countries viewed

Americans. I was raised in a family that was very patriotic, and very proud to be a citizens of the United States. While we were living in St. Lucia, I got my first glimpse of someone from another country having a poor opinion of America. Murray's father immigrated to Canada with his family in his youth. It just so happened that we became friends with some Dutch families who were employed by the nearby Heineken Brewery. Murray was so excited at the prospect of making friends with our Dutch neighbors. And as luck would have it, we were often invited to the same parties. Murray and one of the men would have heated conversations about world affairs. Our friend would say things like he'd rather Holland be occupied by Russia than the American Government, because he didn't trust the United States. I just could not make sense of his reasoning, but accepted that he was entitled to his opinion. What I found interesting was how the two men would disagree vehemently, and go on to discuss other matters in a friendly manner.

I had much the same experience while living in Saudi Arabia. One afternoon several of us stayed after dinner in the Cafeteria to shoot the bull. We started playing a game of "words" that had different meanings in our various homelands. I shouted out a word, and one of the Brits said, "I didn't think they used that term in Canada." I replied that I was from the States, not Canada. He went on to say that if he had known that I was from the States, he wouldn't have ever talked to me in the first place. Wow! That was a low blow. I guess he thought I was Canadian because Murray was, and was therefore friendly to me. I went on to have other such experiences. In the end, I chose to ask questions to find out why such feelings existed. I grew from these experiences, but it was a hard reality. There were times when I got angry or hurt because the explanation for disliking Americans seemed irrational, but there was always something to learn. There were those times, too, when the individual had a good point. I eventually came to realize that I am only responsible for my behavior, and I tried my best to be a good example.

When I returned to Saudi Arabia in 1990, I worked in a five hundred bed hospital in Riyadh. Nurses and support staff were recruited to work at the hospital from nearly forty different countries. I found a family in my coworkers and colleagues, as well as many of the mothers of the patients I cared for. I reported to work the week before the Iraqi invasion of Kuwait, so things were pretty tense for months. The life of an Expat was one of comradery and new experiences, and this time in history provided another layer of complexity.

There were the shopping trips, desert hikes, monthly camping trips, Karate, Pilates, and meeting up at restaurants of every cuisine. Although we lived a fairly sheltered life as an Expat in Saudi Arabia, life was not boring. There were opportunities for every interest if you were willing to explore the city and country with the curiosity of a tourist. Hours were spent with new friends, comparing and contrasting our life experiences, and how we viewed the extraordinary daily occurrences that were not expected when we accepted employment prior to the Gulf Crisis. We from all over the world tried to make sense of what was happening, and what it meant for our individual countries. I was very proud to be an American and grateful for the support we who lived in Saudi Arabia received from the United States.

CHAPTER FOUR
# LIFE OF THE BEDOUIN
DESERT DWELLERS

I gradually learned about Islam while observing my Bedouin patients live out their faith in a disciplined and prayerful manner. We rarely, if ever, spoke of religion, but I witnessed their strict adherence to prayer time, fasting, and praising their God in good times and bad. Being apart of their everyday lives left a lasting impression on me. The women, whom I grew to know so well, seemed to be the same, yesterday, today, and tomorrow. Their character and demeanor rarely wavered. I'd venture to say that life was pretty simple for our Bedouin neighbors devoid of the complexities of a modern world. But, the fact they lived in a fairly harsh environment, without the modern-day conveniences, obviously presented its own challenges. It was clear that their very survival depended on their God,

Allah. Devotion, Discipline, Loyalty, and Reverence are words that come to mind all these years later when I think of my time among the Bedouin. When greeting someone and asking, How are you?" The response was almost always, "I am well," " Alhamdulillah," which meant "Praise God." And when you were parting for the day or night, "Inshallah" meaning "God willing" always accompanied any wish for the future. The phrases became as much a part of me as a result of these encounters as the air I breathed. I found these terms very comforting, and I include them as part of my vocabulary to this day on a fairly regular basis.

The customs and daily routines of those living in the desert, with no electricity or running water in the 20th Century, was such a departure from anything I had previously known. However, having a clear understanding of their way of life was needed to formulate the appropriate nursing care plans for every patient. The majority of our patients had little exposure to the outside world, and many had never been in a hospital or able to avail themselves of medical care in the past. So, it was necessary to find ways to explain the care that was ordered and interpret in a way that made sense.

Oftentimes, there were no words or terms that translated effectively. And, there were often cultural values and customs that interfered with an easy transition. Above all, there was a matter of trust. It was important to address the patient in a way that allowed them to trust their best interest was most important. That was one of my chief motivations for learning enough Arabic to be able to utter the basic greetings or ask or answer simple questions such as "how can I help?" In this way, I think patients developed trust, knowing that I cared enough to communicate with them in their language.

I obviously didn't have a big vocabulary at first, but it was enough to develop a rapport and participate in the conversation when using an interpreter. Everything took longer and some of our practices went against the local customs, so we had to create alternatives. I can't think of a specific example, but I can recall suggesting a very common medical solution or patient care practice to a patient, and hearing the mother or female patient reply, "Haram!" Haram means that it is "not good!" And, if something was Haram, there was no way of talking a patient into it, no matter what the benefit was. So, learning how to provide care and respecting the limitations was like learning a new dance.

Bedouin are nomads who live in the Middle Eastern deserts, including Africa, Israel, and Jordan. Historically, in Saudi Arabia, tribes moved from wadi to wadi, which are valleys in the desert, following the availability of water. The modern Bedouin in Saudi Arabia are more stationery than their ancestors were. When we were living on the KKMC compound, many of our patients lived in their camps year-round because the Saudi Arabian government provided water trucks that held large amounts of water, so they had the security of water available and no longer needed to roam. Our Bedouin neighbors lived in encampments generally housing more than one extended family unit. Each family lived in a large tent, which was where they slept and carried out their daily chores. There was a separate tent for cooking and another just for the men to socialize separated from the women. The woman most often socialized in the cook tent. Goats were raised to feed the family, and there was always a donkey or two to guard the goat against predators. The presence of a Camel was a sign of prosperity.

The patients we cared for in the hospital were primarily our Bedouin neighbors, but we did at times have patients from the Army Corps of Engineers Compound or dependents living on the KKMC Compound. I am certain having access to nearby healthcare extended the life expectancy and quality of life for many who lived in the region and hopefully decreased the infant mortality rate. Individuals were able to easily visit the clinic for prevention and treatment, or be hospitalized when sick, or to deliver a baby. Prior to our hospital being available, medical care was a one to two-hour excursion by car, which was a challenge for most. Most families had access to transportation, but it was still a hardship for most, as it might be for people today. Thankfully, in most instances that was no longer the case. Caring for our patients and getting to know about their culture and customs was a joy, as they were generally very engaging and quite receptive to our being in "their" world.

Prayer and reverence to Allah was the top priority of the Bedouins I knew, which seems to be the practice of many, if not all, practicing Muslims. Loyalty to family, especially one's children, was close behind loyalty to Allah. And, then hospitality and generosity when visiting was evident during the daily visiting hours. If a patient had a visitor, it turned into a tea party for all. It was a very special, fun time. I eventually did my own research and can sum up the Five Pillars of Islam as Faith, Prayer, Charity, Fasting during Ramadan, and Pilgrimage to Mecca during one's lifetime. These practices are what I witnessed while living and working in the Middle East.

Marriages were generally arranged in Saudi Arabia, and many girls were betrothed to a man when they were quite young. Once a girl entered puberty, it was possible for her to marry if the family still approved of the union. When I first reported to work on my new ward, there was a young 14-year-old mother of twin girls on the unit. The twins were delivered prematurely and were too small to be discharged home. Therefore, they resided in the nursery and the mother convalesced in one of our postpartum rooms until they reached their discharge weight. The babies remained in the hospital a week or two after my arrival, so I was able to find out a great deal about Saudi Bedouin customs while she remained in the hospital.

My nurses were great at asking questions about family life, and some were not shy about asking the young mother what it was like to be betrothed and married so young. Our patient's husband was 45, and she shared that they had been married for about a year. She reported that her husband was a kind and caring man and that his age didn't matter to her because of that. I recall him bringing her items to make her hospitalization more tolerable when he came to visit. He brought her special foods that she liked and from time to time a blanket from home or an item of clothing. Of course, he almost always brought pots of tea and coffee and sometimes dates, nuts, or candy. His display of concern was heartwarming, very consistent with how a new father supports the mother of his newborn(s) in the United States.

When the babies were finally able to go home, when weighing 5 pounds, the young mother dressed them in matching pink outfits. The father grinned from cheek to cheek, saying, "Shukran (Thank you), Shukran," as he carried both babies in his arms, and a couple of nurses escorted them to the car. One nurse pushed the mother in a wheelchair, and the other carried the belongings that didn't fit on the young mother's lap. We had great expectations for the two little ones, but it was uncertain how they would fare in the heat of the summer in the tent that was their home. Months later, mother and babies paid us a visit. Each baby was adorned in a pink snowsuit of sorts because it was a cold December that year. Both had chubby cheeks and were in good health. It was a joy and a relief to see that they were doing so well. Thankfully, they never did require readmission to the hospital during my two years at KKMC hospital. What a success story! I credit the excellent care my nurses provided the babies and their mothers, as well as the teaching conversations the young mother received while she was on our ward. However, the young mother was tenacious and determined for her babies to survive, and with the assistance of her husband and extended family, those babies thrived in harsh surroundings. This was a great example for me to witness when I was very new to the area and those who lived there.

Jiddah means grandmother in Arabic, and I met a very special Jiddah while at the KKMC Hospital. Our pediatric patients usually had their mothers with them, but every now and then an older sister might stay with a patient. It was quite unusual to have an older grandmother stay. But there are always exceptions to any norm. Our patient was a young boy, nine or ten years old. He had had a surgery of some sort, and had to remain overnight to make certain he was able to return to his desert home. While making my rounds mid-morning, it was obvious that the woman and her grandson were in the middle of a disagreement. His grandma, or Jiddah, wasn't letting him do what he wanted, so he was trying to overpower her. He was obviously younger and stronger than his grandma, and it appeared he was used to getting his way. When I approached them, I asked what was wrong, and she explained that he didn't want to mind her, and further said that he was handling her in a rough manner. I had never experienced such a thing before. I'm not certain at what point in my contract this occurred, but I'm thinking about a year in when my command of Arabic was adequate. I was able to diffuse the situation at hand but wanted to involve our Social Workers so that the matter might be more thoroughly investigated to make sure the Jiddah was safe in her home.

This was the first time I actually involved our Social Workers in an effort to assess the living environment a patient was discharged to. In this case, we wanted to make sure there was supervision for this child, and that the living environment was safe for the Jiddah. There was a lesson to be learned in this example, but for the most part, I remember that in talking with the parents, it was discovered that the patient was mischievous, and required supervision and discipline. Children were not routinely disciplined, but suggestions were given as to how to guide the child, and impress on him that his Jiddah was asked to stay with him to keep him safe, and he must follow her instructions. I'm not certain how things evolved when they returned home, but at least the matter was broached, and the parents seemed appreciative for the support. Sometimes, when you intercede in a matter and feel you can address the issue as you might in the Western Culture, you may make the problem worse instead of solving it. That's why I immediately involved our Saudi Social Workers. I had learned, while living in St. Lucia, that my way of assessing an issue doesn't necessarily translate in another culture, and my solution may not work in my new country.

For my intercession on her behalf and supporting her in gaining control of her grandson, the Jiddah gave me a gold ring to show her appreciation. The ring was Bedouin folk art, featuring an etched tree of some sort. I declined initially, but she kept insisting. She saw me as an ally because I promised to protect her by asking my staff to keep an eye on her grandson until their discharge. And, she was grateful that the Social Workers would follow up with her when she went home. It was a very unusual case, one such I never encountered again.

I have such fond memories of this little Jiddah. I cherished that ring for years until I found the right person to give it to. I love passing down jewelry and stories. I have given almost all the pieces of jewelry I've been given over the years to friends and family and shared the stories that made them special. I think it's a lovely practice. Ok, you guessed it. I'm a regifter. What a beautiful way to share yourself with others; unless you're re-gifting something you don't like. That's what Goodwill or St. Vincent DePaul are for.

Murray and I had been working at the KKMC hospital for about nine months when we received an invitation for dinner at the residence of one of the Saudi Ambulance drivers. We were amongst several other couples from the hospital who received the same invitation, doctors and various department heads and their spouses. These outings were always fun, in more ways than one. Of course, it was always an adventure to visit a Bedouin Camp, because you never knew what was going to happen, or what you might witness. Living in the desert was often quite unpredictable. I'll never forget what happened during our first visit to a Bedouin Camp; in fact, I have a couple of photos displayed in my home that I took that day. It is fun to remember the time I will never forget.

We traveled about thirty minutes from our compound into the desert. I had never visited a Bedouin camp, so had no idea whatsoever to expect. Our host eagerly met us as our group began to vacate the transport, and accompanied us to an area infant of the tents. Two small girls ran up to us and eventually joined our host, who appeared to be their father, near a goat tethered to a pole. The goat had been prepared for slaughter, and our host indicated to us that this would be performed today in honor of our visit. As I would learn, it was customary to slaughter the animal to be prepared for the meal in the presence of guests, as a guarantee to the freshness of the meat. Well, that was quite the event, to say the least. A machete was used to cut the goat's throat, and the process was quick and without a struggle. Our host's two young girls stood waiting expectantly nearby. As soon as the process was completed, they ran up to their father waiting for their "prize." Each girl was given one of the testicles, which served as a toy ball. They ran off swinging them in the air, and were no longer interested in our activities. Over the years of traveling abroad, I found that children living in remote regions often made toys out of what they could find readily in nature or discarded by the adults in their families. Pretty inventive!

Soon after our initiation to Bedouin life, our group was separated and ushered into different tents. The women and children spent the afternoon in what was designated the women's tent, and the men were entertained in the tent designated for men only. Most of the women from our compound were in the country as dependents and didn't work, and had limited experience conversing in Arabic. My Arabic was very rudimentary at the time, but I knew enough to utter a few sentences that could get a response and a bit of laughter from time to time. As we waited for dinner to be served, we communicated in a sign language of sorts, actually more like playing a game of charades. I knew a little Arabic but soon realized that many of the words used commonly in the hospital weren't exactly helpful in a social situation. It's not often you ask someone if they have pain, or need to go to use the restroom or tell them it's time to take their medicine when you are at a party. So, we smiled a lot and laughed when a word of Arabic or English was spoken and understood by all in attendance.

As we were sitting and socializing, the wife of our host quickly rose from where she was seated and ran out of the tent. A donkey had gotten into a small supply tent, and the next thing we saw was a donkey being chased away from the tent by our hostess. Honestly, I found it quite entertaining, as did the other women from our compound, but the lady of the "house" was not at all amused. She soon returned to our tent and we spent the rest of the day without incident. She joined us and we sat in a circle around the refreshments most of the day. Most informal gatherings featured Arabic coffee and tea, as well as dates and maybe an assortment of nuts. The tea was very sweet and the coffee was brewed with cardamom; I'd say it was an "acquired taste." I found sipping the tea or coffee slowly made it possible to acquire the taste over time. It was important to always eat and drink what was served, no matter whether it was something you thought you'd like or not. It seems you can eat and drink most anything in small calculated bites. This is a good habit to form if and when you may plan to travel outside your comfort zone.

Eventually, dinner was ready. The goat had been roasted over an open fire, and when dinner was served, our portion of the goat and cooked rice was brought to us on a big bronze platter. It was apparent that women and children were served the innards, or organ meats, and smaller pieces of the goat. I guess the men were served the larger portions of the animal. Oh well, it didn't bother me. I can't remember what I ate, but it was good. We were participating in what was called a "goat grab." All in attendance sat on the floor, grabbed at the meat and rice, and then ate with our hands. That definitely wouldn't work in today's world, but most if not all of the women who joined me from KKMC ate at least a small portion of the meal. Before long, we were reunited with our husbands and offered our thanks and appreciation for a lovely afternoon. It truly was a wonderful time. I was grateful to have been able to converse and be understood, if only minimally. Air kisses and hugs ensued, and we were soon off across the desert back home.

Visiting the Bedouin camp, witnessing the slaughter of the goat, and partaking in a meal together was like participating in a team-building event. Those of us who were invited to dinner that day bonded as a workgroup does when spending the day at an indoor rock wall to build team spirit. We had all witnessed and engaged in an activity that you may only understand by being a part of it. The friends I made that day became good friends, and we would kibitz about that time together whenever we ran into one another on the compound. There were always one or two individuals who shared the experience in much the same way, which led to an interesting conversation on the way home on the bus, and further cemented the chance for a long-term friendship. I loved the time spent riding in the bus while on these outings. They brought back fond memories of school field trips and various church and club trips out of town, playing games, singing, and goofing around. The kid in me loved these outings on the bus!

Over the years, I developed the habit of making rounds on all my patients with either their incoming or outgoing nurses at the change of shift. This practice was a great way to get a sense of the patient's condition while having the nurse available to answer questions or verify orders prior to leaving the ward. As Head Nurse, I continued this practice, and it was a discipline I introduced to the ward I managed while at KKMC. One morning during rounds, I entered the room of a very ill child, who was not quite a year old. I believe the child had meningitis, and the prognosis was poor. The mother was at the bedside, and as I approached her we shared the usual greeting, "Salam A Lakum," "Alakem Salam," This greeting was basically a very formal way to say "Hello." Since the situation was quite grave, I no doubt spoke in a reserved manner. After our initial exchange, I asked her how she was, "Kaif Halak?"

Her response, much to my surprise, was "Alhumdulallah," "Praise God." I was incredulous. "Doesn't this mother know how sick her child is?" I thought to myself. In talking with her further, it was obvious that she did not know how sick her child was, but she also knew it was out of her control, and it appeared that she was giving the outcome to God. Incredible!

Since that time, and that encounter, I have never been the same. The faith of that woman has challenged my faith all these years later. At that moment, I had a difficult time imagining the level of trust and admiration she had for her God. She offered praises to Him, saying "Alhumdullalah", and turning things over to him saying "Inshaahlah," meaning God willing, in the face of her child's critical condition. It has been over 30 years since that morning, and I have never forgotten her response, nor her demeanor. In the midst of such trauma and pending grief, her response was "Thanks be to God." As I said, I have never been the same since that day. The woman's response deepened my faith and made me a stronger believer.

This example of trust and devotion to Allah was perhaps the most striking, but I heard this same exaltation and sentiment over and over during the years I was living and working in Saudi Arabia, whether in Hafar Al Batin or in Riyadh. I may have mentioned elsewhere in the book that many of my friends thought the sayings were rote, more a habit or matter of fact. My perception was quite different, especially after living in the harsh desert and witnessing so many women rely on Allah for the care of their children. The Bedouin were uneducated, and the majority were unable to read, so it was difficult for many to understand exactly what was being told to them about their sick or injured child. The response most often, if not always was "Inshaahlah" when told the type of treatment recommended. I explain it as one having blind faith. And, as I said, it was very inspiring to me to witness on a regular basis.

It was a quiet day in the Women and Children's Ward when a call came out over the loudspeaker requesting all available personnel to report to the Emergency Room immediately. I went to the ER with a couple of my nurses, and much to our dismay there were several injured children lying on cots, crying, and hospital staff on a mission to address the severely injured first and then attend to those with more minor injuries. All available staff readily started taking vital signs and thoroughly assessing the various injuries. In time, it was determined that most injuries were minor, but one child sustained more serious injuries and was in a coma.

A School Bus carrying children returning home for the day was traveling on the highway just outside of Hafar Al Batin, when it collided with an oncoming car. Thankfully, the highway was well-traveled, and emergency services were immediately notified of the accident. School Buses didn't have seat belts in those days, and by all accounts, the children were violently tossed about within the vehicle. The possibility of a school bus accident threw me for a loop, as I didn't even know that Hafar Al Batin had schools, let alone school buses.

As I said, most of the children were not seriously injured and were able to be discharged home. We admitted several children that required overnight observation and there were a few who would remain with us for a while because of fractures requiring surgery and post-operative stabilization. As I mentioned, one child remained in a coma, and he was admitted to our ICU room on the floor. Our ward had the capacity for 30 patients, and one of the rooms was designated for those requiring intensive care. If a patient required more advanced care than we could provide, they were transferred to a hospital in Riyadh or Dhahran. We had a top-notched Pediatrician from Montreal, Canada for a good part of my two years at KKMC. Because of his well-rounded knowledge and expertise, we generally cared for our critical patients and rarely transferred them out. Hospitalization in another part of the country was very hard on the family and the patient, so we did our best to care for them without the necessity of a transfer. Our pediatric patients were blessed to have such talented doctors and excellent nurses providing their care. It was truly a privilege to be a part of this team.

The boy who was admitted to the ICU suite remained in a coma for days. He was stable in that his vital signs were within normal limits and he was breathing on his own, but he remained unresponsive. He otherwise appeared neurologically intact on examination, when assessing his reflexes and the ability to easily manipulate his limbs without restriction or spasms. So, we waited and observed, and developed a plan for when, and if, he should be transferred to a hospital where the child could be further assessed by specialists. His parents grew weary waiting for him to wake up. His name was Karim, and he was 11 years old, the oldest of his parents' children. They were devastated as they watched him, unchanged, day after day. Later in the afternoon of the third or fourth day of his hospitalization, I was making rounds with our doctor, and the parents wanted to talk with us about Karim's treatment plan. They patiently listened as the doctor explained that it appeared that Karim was quite stable, and there was no clear explanation for his remaining comatose. He suggested caring for Karim for a day or two more in our hospital, and if there was no improvement after that, the boy would be transferred to a more advanced facility.

The parents looked at their son, and then returned their gaze to us, and what followed was quite surprising. The mother spoke for both her and her husband in a very strong and capable manner, when she spoke her husband would nod in agreement. She told us that her family was accustomed to call upon a "Spiritual Healer" to conduct a ritual for recovery from an illness or injury. The mother further explained that the child's head would be shaved and then cabbage leaves would be placed on his head. Our doctor listened intently and then requested some time to consider what the parents had requested of him. We retreated to the Nurse's Station and discussed what had just been relayed to us. By all accounts, it seemed crazy to think that what the mother was suggesting would help at all. The child had been receiving all the care that was deemed indicated for his condition, and he remained unconscious. What was a treatment of cabbage leaves on a shaved head going to do? Well, our pediatrician decided that there was nothing to lose. However, when he spoke with the parents and agreed that the Healer should be summoned for the ritual, it was decided that the child would be transferred to a higher level of care hospital if the treatment did not yield the hoped-for results.

So, the Spiritual Healer arrived that evening, and the child's head was shaved, and the cabbage leaves were placed. I do believe an herb or substance of some sort was rubbed on the scalp prior to the placement of cabbage leaves. The Medicine man stayed with the child the entire time, closely observing him and making certain the head remained covered with the cabbage leaves. The Healer remained next to the child's bed, as he read from the Koran and prayerfully attended the young boy. The boy's parents remained in the room, in silent observance of the man in attendance, praying for a miracle. The hours passed, and on the morning of the second day, the healer removed the cabbage leaves, and to our amazement, there was a small shaft of hair emerging right on the top of the child's bald head. As was described as part of the treatment, a hot ember was used by the Healer to burn the hair that emerged. When the ritual was completed, the man left the room and did not return. The boy remained sleeping, and the parents watched and prayed. Late that afternoon, the mother came running out the room, "Tal, Tal," which meant "Come, Come." We went running into the room, and much to our immense surprise, Karim was waking up. He seemed pretty confused, but he woke up! Oh my goodness, to this day I don't know what to say. Perhaps, he was going to wake up anyway, I don't know. No one knows. But, he did wake up and did not seem to have any major deficits. He and his mother remained with us for another few days, and then he was discharged home, never to be seen again. OMG!

## Chapter Five
# LIFE IN THE DESERT
### Always an Adventure

Upon arrival, integration into our private and work lives on the King Khalid Medical City compound was quite abrupt. We had waited for weeks to reach our new work home, and the staff at KKMC had by all accounts been anxiously awaiting our arrival. It was apparent that they were eager to have a permanent Head Nurse of the Women and Children's Ward and a Family Practice Physician to fill vacant shifts in the clinic and Emergency Room. When we finally were deposited on the doorstep of the hospital that June morning in 1982, it seemed our Welcoming Committee, Mohammed Ali and his colleague Sultan, knew all about us and were eager to introduce us to their hospital. Mohammed Ali took particular pride in the fact that he shared his namesake with the famous

American Boxer. He was quite outgoing, where his colleague Sultan was soft-spoken and appeared somewhat shy. So, it was safe to say that Mohammed Ali did the majority of the talking that day as we were introduced to the hospital and many of the key personnel.

Mohammed Ali and Sultan were the hospital's Social Workers, and they became my right-hand men. Their assistance was absolutely necessary to succeed in my job. They functioned as a living dictionary and encyclopedia, which I desperately needed when communicating essential information to patients and their families, and in the delivery of safe nursing care. I needed these men to explain to me the customs of their country as they related to the nursing care my staff would render. Mohammed Ali and Sultan not only assisted when I needed an interpreter, they provided me with daily on-the-job training in regards to learning essential Hospital Arabic. They were extremely respectful and patient, although, over time, their patience was tried from at times in working with an impatient nurse (me) at times. At times, the men found themselves in a tough spot between myself and a patient, because modern nursing care didn't always translate easily within a culture that hadn't yet entered the 20th Century. However, we were able to meet in the middle, or close, and manage to provide exceptional care.

A situation that required their expert attention was when the mother of a child who required isolation had an infant who was breastfeeding. It was near impossible for the child to remain home without the mother, because there was generally no refrigeration in the home, and no one to feed the baby in her absence. The Bedouin women were quite social, and while in the hospital enjoyed spending time with the other mothers. Our Social Workers needed to relay a message to the mother in isolation that she would not be able to visit the other mothers while her child was hospitalized. This was not a favorite conversation for either of our social workers. They preferred we handle communicating this message to the mothers. However, it was so important that the message be communicated accurately, that I did not want to take the chance of not being understood. The two men not only were able to interpret the important message, they had the clout needed to uphold the policy if questioned. This is a perfect example of a time when Mohammed Ali or Sultan might have become a bit terse with me. I guess, over time, they expected me to have a better command of Arabic. But, they learned that even if my command of the language was quite good, I would always request an interpreter to convey information that was important to the patient's recovery and safety. We did have an interpreter, Suliman, who was available for our ward six eight-hour shifts a week. He was only one man, though, and was often busy translating for another nurse, when an urgent situation arose. Thus, the need for Mohammed and Sultan. Over time, we were assigned another interpreter, and by that time, the need for Mohammed Ali and Sultan was less, and for that they seemed grateful.

My nursing staff was pretty creative in caring for our patients for the year we had but one Arabic interpreter designated specifically for our unit. I have nothing but words of praise for my Nursing Staff and Social Workers during that year. Luckily, our interpreter Suliman, a mild-mannered gentleman from Sudan, was an excellent worker, and able to do the job of two on most days. He was a gentleman in every sense of the word, and his demeanor allowed him to work on the floor designated for women and children only. His job was a delicate one, which he managed in a very respectful, kind, and gentle manner. He was crucial to the effectiveness of our work, especially when communicating very important information to our female population. As a man, he needed to tread carefully, with the utmost respect. Suliman was Muslim, so he understood the religious practice of Islam, and because he had worked in Saudi Arabia for several years, he was able to assist our patient population in a way that was comfortable for the majority of our patients.

Suliman taught me about the Islamic religion and how it related to my Christian faith. I will never forget the day we were sitting at the nurses' station, he was reading a newspaper, as I was reviewing charts and confirming that all the orders had been carried out. It must have been a slow day, maybe a Friday, which is like a Sunday in America. The majority of our patients had visitors on what was "the weekend," which provided a little downtime for the staff, unless of course there were really ill patients. As Suliman read the Arabic newspaper he held in his hand, he read out loud the headline he was focused on. As he finished, he asked me, "Is it true that most people in the US are Jewish?" "What?" I said. "Of course not. Where did you hear that?" "That's what I read in another magazine or newspaper I recently was reading," he said. We bantered back and forth for some time, as I assured him that there were many of Jewish faith living in New York and Florida, but that there were many states where the numbers were quite low. To be sure, I didn't really know these numbers, but I was certain that that statement was not true.

That question and my retort led to quite a lengthy explanation by Suliman regarding Islam and its origin. I admitted that I really didn't know much about Islam, and was very interested in learning. He went on to explain that Ishmael was the son of Abraham, who was Abraham's wife Sara's handmaid Hagar's child. Abraham is thought to be the Father of the Christian and Jewish faiths. And, the fact that Ishmael is known as a prophet and an ancestor to Muhammed, Abraham is the Father of Islam, too. In 1983, I guess I was not well informed about the Islamic religion, and I did not know that the Jewish, Christian and Islamic faiths all descended from the same origin, and that Abraham was ultimately the father of all. I had known

Suliman for well over a year when we had this discussion, and we seemed to have a respect for one another and could converse in a spirit of cooperation. This type of conversation could have been awkward, but we were able to educate each other where we experienced a lack of knowledge or understanding. It was a beautiful exchange, and one that deepened my understanding of the world I lived in. I do think the respect we held for each other somehow grew after our conversation that day.

Suliman was incredible. He had lived and worked in Saudi Arabia for years prior to my arrival on the ward at KKMC, and seemed to have a good understanding of the Bedouin culture and people. He was extremely sensitive and caring, and he interpreted exactly what was said, which is not always the case with interpreters. I say this because very often interpreters paraphrase or summarize what is being said; Suliman did not, which was very important and increased his value as an interpreter. As I began to better understand Arabic, this was very obvious. Everybody knew that he was a very devout Muslim. He prayed during every prayer call and displayed tremendous discipline during Ramadan and all Religious Holidays. He had a very gentle and respectful spirit and received much respect and care from coworkers and other hospital personnel because of his character.

I hate to admit that I didn't even know where Sudan was. Sometime after my first year at KKMC, Suliman went back to Sudan for his Home Leave. The Home Leave that we were given during our two-year contract was a four-week paid leave, including airfare back to our country of origin. Many of the individuals who then were referred to as "Third Country Nationals" generally did not take their other leaves, saving money to travel back home, often bringing numerous gifts for the entire family. Suliman took his leave and went home for a month. Unfortunately, he was not able to return back to Saudi Arabia as planned because a civil war broke out while he was home. The Second Sudanese Civil War was a conflict that began in 1983 and ended in 2005. By all accounts, it was largely a continuation of the First Sudanese Civil War from 1955-1972. I couldn't believe what he had to go through to return to Saudi Arabia. He had to walk many miles, travel by train, boat, and ultimately air.

I only realized over the past many years the significance of what Suliman experienced and endured to return to Saudi Arabia, to his job, and to the life he developed outside his home country and away from his family. I can't imagine back in the 80s, traveling home to visit and having travel plans upset by a Civil War. But, those were more carefree days for Americans, unlike many citizens of other countries. There have been many disruptions over the years that have made life challenging for many.

Sometime during the last several months of my contract in 1984, Suliman took his leave and made a pilgrimage to Mecca. A Muslim is expected to make a pilgrimage to Mecca once in a lifetime unless a health issue or absolute inability to travel to Mecca prohibits it. It is customary that if a Muslim is not able to make a pilgrimage during the yearly Haj, they can make it at another time. As I said, Suliman was extremely devout in the practice of his religion. He was so excited to make his pilgrimage for a three-day observance in Mecca. On his return, there was something different about him. His behavior was very odd, and he said things that just didn't make sense. It was determined that he had a psychosis that at times affects those on a religious pilgrimage. Suliman was placed on antipsychotic medication, but he didn't like the effect. At the time I returned home after the completion of my contract, Suliman was admitted to the hospital for stabilization. My prayer was that he would recover and be able to return to work. To this day, I do not know what happened to my friend Suliman, but I pray he has had a good life, which he richly deserves.

Every day was an adventure from the time I first stepped foot on Saudi soil. I never knew what to expect when I walked through the doors of the KKMC hospital. The customs and culture of my patients were so unique that I had to rely extensively on the nurses and interpreters who had been in the country for several months, if not years, before my arrival. One morning on my arrival to the unit, there was a new patient who seemed very familiar to the staff, talking on the telephone in the Nurse's Station. She appeared to know her way around the ward, as well as what was expected of her as a patient. What struck me was how assertive this woman was, and the assurance in which she conducted herself. I had read about and had been told that the Saudi Arabian women, especially Bedouin, were quite reserved and most often deferred to their husbands when in an unfamiliar setting. This woman was hospitalized due to a female problem she struggled with. She had previously been diagnosed with endometriosis and was hospitalized due to excessive bleeding, and the severe pain related to the condition. This young woman was unable to have children, which I was told was grounds for divorce in Saudi Arabia.

When I arrived on the ward that morning, our patient was on the phone insisting that her husband visit and bring some items from home as soon as possible. It appeared that he was quite devoted to her, as he arrived on the ward later that morning, carrying the items she requested. Over the two years I worked at the hospital on the KKMC Compound, the Sergeant's wife Layla was admitted two or three other times. During this time, she announced that her husband was taking another wife, but that she would always be number one. This appeared to be true. For, although she was unable to bear her husband a child, his devotion and loyalty never seemed to waver. I was so impressed with this woman. She seemed to have a strength within her to state what she wanted and which course of treatment she preferred. She was very adamant that she was in charge of her body, and that she would have the final say on what treatment she would receive, but she relied on her husband for support.

The last time Layla was hospitalized, she told us that her husband had received a transfer and that they would be moving. She did mention that her husband had taken a second wife, but that she remained wife #1, and that she would help the second wife integrate into the family, and that they would be friends. She made it clear that her husband loved her, but that he deserved to have children. I think this was a very unusual situation, but unusual is often good. And, it was good to know that it is not always true that in Saudi Arabia a husband will divorce a wife if she is unable to have children. Perhaps other statements about the Bedouin or Saudi Arabian Nationals were untrue. I love exceptions to the rules, making room for anything to happen, no matter what has happened in the past.

Days later, we admitted a woman accompanied by her husband, who was very neatly dressed in a spotless, pressed garment. Our new patient was wearing a crisp black abaya (cover) and was carrying a fancy make-up case. This was really quite unusual because most of our patients lived in the desert, and regular washing and pressing of clothing was not part of desert living. Patients usually brought with them a minimum of belongings when they were admitted to the hospital. Not only was she carrying a cute little make-up case, but her husband was also carrying a full-size suitcase with the belongings she would need during her hospital stay. "What on earth was she bringing with her?" I thought to myself. While doing the admission interview, it was unearthed that our patient was the wife of the Mayor of Hafar Al Batin. I didn't even know Hafar Al Batin had a mayor. But, I came to realize that although the region was very remote and seemingly undeveloped, it was very much on the map, and its own municipality. The town of Hafar Al Batin had a mayor, schools with a bus service, and a fairly busy trading center. Hafar Al Batin even had a sit down restaurant. Once again, I learned to never judge a book by its cover.

The Mayor's wife was quick to don an apricot nightgown, which she wore for a day, changing into a different one for every day of her hospital stay. She was scheduled to have a series of tests to help determine the root cause of the stomach trouble she had been experiencing. During her stay, she had a laparoscopy and was able to be discharged home fairly quickly. Throughout her brief hospital stay, she was eager to educate us on what her life was like, and how her life differed from the average Saudi Arabian citizen. Talking to the Mayor's wife proved to be quite interesting. She spent hours talking to the other women and made an effort to entertain the nursing staff when they entered her room. She shared cookies, candies, teas, and coffee whenever a nurse provided care or medication. I have a photo of her in her apricot nightgown, with her head cover in place, holding two pieces of fruit. She made an effort to look "the part" when posing for the photo. She seemed to enjoy every moment of her hospital stay. She initially attempted to throw her weight around because she was the mayor's wife. But, eventually, she realized that myself and my staff treated all our patients with equal amounts of respect and kindness, and there was no need for name-dropping. I have to say this was such a perfect example of the tremendous staff I worked within that tiny KKMC Hospital so many years ago.

The Mayor's wife seemed a bit pretentious, but her husband appeared very reserved and down to earth. I learned a long time ago that it is important to be open-minded, especially when in a new situation. There is a good chance things may not be as they appeared. This has been true of so many of my life experiences. Often I have heard or may have read that a place I am visiting or its residents are known to be a certain way, but then I have a totally different experience than expected. I am happy that life is like that, because I like to make my own assessment before forming an opinion. Wouldn't it be boring if life was predictable?

Sometime during our first year at KKMC, my husband and one of the other ER doctors were given a car to share. Having a car at our disposal was an absolute luxury, making it a little easier to get around the compound, and take trips off-compound. It was so fun to leave the compound on our days off and go exploring; whether or not that was a good idea, I'm not so sure. One weekend, we decided to go on a road trip with a friend who worked in the ER with Murray. We were all excited to visit the famous sand dunes near the town of Zilfi. People were always raving about the awesome pictures these dunes made if taken at the right time of the day. I'm not completely sure what we were thinking, as I was about six months pregnant, and in 1983 there were no cell phones. We didn't even know if there was a good hospital in the region. Oh, the days of carefree living, not a worry in the world.

We took off for Zilfi early in the morning and arrived at our destination by midday. In attempting to pull over to the side of the road to take photos of the famous sand dunes, our car got mired in the soft sand. We were stuck, and could not manage to get enough traction beneath the wheels to get out. Luckily, a couple of men came to our rescue and managed to set us free. One of the men was a local police officer and the other was originally from Syria but was working on a local engineering project in Zilfi. The Syrian gentleman spoke fairly good English, and before we knew it we were invited to the policeman's home for lunch. When we arrived at his home, my guys were invited to ride one of their horses, while I befriended the resident camel. I had a photo taken of myself and the camel. I later copied that photo as letterhead for stationery and used it to announce my pregnancy to family and friends back in the States. What a fun experience.

When we arrived at their home, I was introduced to the Policeman's wife, but then was asked to join my husband and friend for the meal. It is customary for the women to eat and socialize in one part of the house, while the men gather in another part of the house. For some reason, the Saudi policeman said that it was okay for me to remain with my husband in the room with them. Because I did speak some Arabic and understood more than I could speak, I knew what the policeman was saying to me. Our host did not speak English, so he asked the Syrian gentleman to interpret for him and for us. It appeared to me that the questions he wanted the Syrian gentleman to ask me were really quite forward, and he seemed to rarely interpret what was being asked, out of politeness. Thankfully, the wife must have requested that I join her in the kitchen, so I was allowed to leave the male gathering. I did not let on that I was uncomfortable, for I didn't want there to be any trouble.

I remember the Policeman's wife being kind, and appearing to make every effort to help me feel comfortable. She was interested in the fact I was expecting a child and was able to share about her baby, who happened to be sleeping during our visit. When visiting anywhere, especially when there is not a language in common, it's always a blessing to have a subject in common. I knew enough Arabic that I could ask her the age and sex of her child and if her parents lived nearby. I was able to tell her when the baby was due, and that I was a nurse who took care of children. Those subjects filled the bulk of an hour or so. Today, all you'd have to do is pull out your phone and show pictures, and find an Arabic Interpreter app to talk for you. Who knows which is best?

Finally, it was time to leave, so Murray and our friend went to get the car. As I was saying goodbye to my new friend, her husband arrived just as I walked out the kitchen door. Much to my surprise, he approached me as I stood in the doorway, and kissed me on the lips. I was so taken by surprise, I didn't know what to do but so I hurried to the waiting car. I did not tell my husband what just happened, for fear of what he might do. I just wanted to get out of there as quickly as possible, and that we did. We had been invited to return again soon, but when I told my husband what had occurred, that possibility was out of the question. I was relieved that we didn't exchange our contact information with them.

When I returned to work the next day, I told the Canadian obstetrician I worked with about the strange occurrence. His response was a bit unexpected. He said, "in the Saudi Arabian culture, a married woman, especially one with child, would never venture out uncovered, in the company of men." When a Western woman goes about her business uncovered, the culture interprets this behavior as "being easy." In the future, I made certain I covered if we were in a rural town, where customs are adhered to more strictly, and especially if we visited a Saudi's private home. I take responsibility for my ignorance or disrespect in adhering to the local customs or practice of Islam. However, the policeman's behavior was inexcusable and thankfully was not a common occurrence in the years I spent living and traveling in the Middle East.

It is so important to respect the culture you are living or traveling in. It seems to be a very American thing to want to impose our freedoms and customs on the country we are visiting. This is a totally different situation, but nonetheless, demonstrated how necessary it is to respect the culture and customs of the host country. Murray and I traveled to China in 1983, visiting lesser-known cities then, such as Kunming, Canton, and Chongqing, Chengdu, and Wuhan. In explaining where we might eat, our tour guide provided some recommendations, specifically those restaurants which were best for visitors. He made a point to tell us that there were some excellent traditional Chinese restaurants that were specifically for locals, but if foreign travelers entered the restaurants, the locals would immediately evacuate the premises. It was a cultural thing, many of the local people were not comfortable eating in the presence of foreigners. In 1982, tourism was still quite new in the cities outside Beijing and Shanghai, so we obviously adhered to this advice. Similar suggestions were provided in other countries, and I know it is important to heed these guidelines. My experience in Zilfi reminded me of this, and my husband and I made sure I socialized only in the company of women while visiting in the future, no matter what.

# PEOPLE OF ISLAM

## Chapter Six
## IN TRANSITION
### A Lifetime of Change

Our baby was on the way and Murray had been accepted into the Emergency Medicine Residency at the University of Maryland in Baltimore for July of 1984. Although we both enjoyed living and working in Saudi Arabia, we had decided sometime into our second year to leave when the terms of our 2-year contract were satisfied. Murray wanted to pursue more education in Emergency Medicine and was excited about starting the Residency. Since we wanted to be closer to our families after the baby was born, moving back to the United States for more training would make that possible. As our time in Saudi Arabia came to an end, we prepared ourselves for the challenges and need for flexibility on the horizon. Change and being flexible seemed to be a constant in the lifestyle we had grown accustomed to.

The second week in April was my projected due date, and although I was allowed six weeks of Maternity Leave, I still needed to go back to work for several weeks to finish my contract. The time came to arrange childcare, but I didn't know where to begin. As luck or fate would have it, the perfect person for the position was a nurse working in my ward. Fatma was an excellent prospect, but would she be open to the opportunity, and would it be okay with the Hospital Administration? She loved babies, and thankfully, was very open to the possibility of helping us out. We were able to get clearance from the administration for Fatma to adjust her work schedule to accommodate my schedule, as well as Murray's. Although I was Fatma's superior, we had a mutual respect for each other, and genuinely liked one another. When all was said and done, having Fatma take care of our infant while we were working was the perfect solution.

Fatma had been working at the KKMC Hospital for four years prior to my arrival in 1982, and was an experienced Medical/Surgical and Pediatric Nurse, in addition to being a Nurse Midwife. Because her IV skills were impeccable, I often relied on her if I needed help with an IV. Don't get me wrong, my other nurses had excellent skills, but for some reason, Fatma and I had an easy rapport. She was a gifted nurse and a wonderful friend. Originally from Turkey, Arabic was Fatma's native tongue. Although she was not a practicing Muslim, she had been raised in a Muslim home and understood the Islamic religion practiced by the majority of our patients. In addition to being a hard-working and loyal nurse, Fatma was an individual I felt I could trust. Because of this, I was able to put my complete faith in her to care for my newborn when it was time for me to go back to work. My friend Joe uses a phrase when describing a person whose character is stable and dependable. He would say "She's like a one-way street." What you see is what you get. Knowing Fatma was a one-way street was very reassuring since I had to work for another six weeks after my six-week Maternity Leave to complete my contract. She not only managed to cover our work schedules over those six weeks but also took excellent care of Gerrit. He always seemed so content with Fatma, and rarely fussy while in her care. She would bring

Gerrit to the hospital for his feedings, and then we would pick him up at her residence after work. When the time came, it was very hard to say goodbye.

We stayed in contact with each other after we both returned to our home countries; Fatma to Turkey and Murray, Gerrit, and I to the States. We eventually settled in New York, and Fatma settled in Ankara, Turkey. We talked often on the phone and remained in contact until I returned to Saudi Arabia years later and visited her in Turkey. I remember her saying that her folks were upset with her because she continued to live alone, independently. Her parents held traditional Muslim beliefs and believed that an unmarried woman should live with her family. Fatma had been independent too long and didn't go along with that thinking. Apparently, this caused her to be estranged from her parents for a while. From what Fatma shared, it was hard on her to return to Turkey because of the strict rules for unmarried women. However, travel in the Middle East became quite treacherous at times, and it seemed that Fatma wanted what appeared to be a more stable environment. I remember receiving a call from Fatma when she was traveling home to Turkey through Lebanon sometime between 1982 and 1983. She was in the Beirut airport transferring planes and there were explosions in the airport, I could actually hear on the phone. She wanted me to know what was happening in case she didn't make it home to her parents, and they called the hospital wondering where she was. I was left speechless when later pondering the significance of what she was enduring. Fatma did make it home and was eventually able to return to Saudi Arabia without incident. However, I do believe that the experience overshadowed any thought of returning for another two-year contract. She was ready to go home, where there would be no need to travel through potentially dangerous regions of the world.

We had a busy last month in Saudi Arabia prior to our return home to the United States. We made trips to the American Consulate in Dhahran to register Gerrit's American Birth Certificate, and then to Riyadh for Gerrit's Passport Photos needed to apply for his U.S. Passport a week or so later. I can't remember if we flew or drove to Al Khobar, but know it was a six-hour car ride to Khobar, and I know we drove to Riyadh, which was at least a five-hour drive. Nonetheless, that's a lot of driving for a passport, but we were full of excitement and expectation, so all in all, a true labor of love! It's funny, when I think back to our time in Saudi Arabia over those two years, I took everything in stride, and looked at life as fairly normal. I failed to realize at the time that what we were living through was really quite remarkable, and notable, and not the least bit ordinary. I think that we had had so many new experiences in such a fairly short period of time, that the extraordinary seemed ordinary.

Throughout most of my pregnancy, once my baby bump was visible, I received much attention and well-wishing for a safe delivery on a daily basis. As Head Nurse of the unit, I interacted with all the patients and their families pretty extensively. If a patient was in the hospital for any length of time, we usually developed a nice rapport and enjoyed spending time together throughout the day. It was very common for my female patients or mothers of pediatric patients to hug me and even shower me with kisses, especially during my pregnancy. I received prayers for myself and my baby that Allah would watch over us, and that I would be blessed with a son. I noticed girls being received very happily, but it was an extreme honor in the eyes of the Bedouin to have the firstborn be a son. Well, obviously, my husband and I wanted a healthy baby, with no preference to sex, but when Gerrit turned out to be a boy, there was much celebration on the part of our Saudi patients and coworkers. It was a lovely experience to be prayed for, and I was often told that there was a place for me in Heaven for my good deeds on earth. I mention this only because this was so common, weekly in fact.

The last week in June of 1984, we were on our way home on Saudi/Pan Am Airlines. The flight was thirteen-hours to New York City, but, by the time we reached my parents' home in Wisconsin, we were in an airplane or airport for a total of twenty-seven hours after leaving Dhahran International Airport. Gerrit was an excellent traveler, and by all accounts still is. On our arrival in Wisconsin, we packed the car we had had in storage for the past 3 years and began our trek to Baltimore to begin the next leg of our life's journey. We arrived in Baltimore just before the 4th of July, and were able to witness fireworks in the Baltimore Harbor, and later visit Fort McHenry, where Francis Scott Key was reported to have written the Star-

Spangled Banner. Murray transitioned to the Emergency Medicine Program well, far better than I did without friends or a work-life. We eventually rented a home in a kid-friendly neighborhood, and life started to fall into place.

If you have ever lived abroad, even traveled abroad, it is often a lonely experience. Friends and family may be interested in your pictures and a Reader's Digest version of your experiences, but after that, you're pretty much on your own. We were warned of this phenomenon and found it to be very true. We didn't know anyone else who had worked in Saudi Arabia, but one of the second year ER residents had been a volunteer in St. Lucia at the same time as us, so having her there made our transition a little smoother than it might have been. Having any familiarity when you move to a new place, whether in the States or internationally is a plus. Thankfully, I was also able to make friends with other mothers of infants, so we had something in common, and I tried to put my life in Saudi Arabia behind me and integrate into the American Dream I had left years before.

Life was good, and we were making friends and memories in Maryland, and then the dreaded letter accompanied Murray home one day. For whatever reason, the University of Maryland was losing its accreditation and funding for the Emergency Medicine Residency Program the following year. This loss of status meant that if Murray were to finish his training in Baltimore, his credentials would not carry the same weight as from an Accredited Program. This may be important when vying for a coveted position against other worthy applicants, but may not really mean anything in the long run. But, receiving strong credentials from a good program was important to Murray. We were again at a crossroads. Then, the most unexpected thing happened; an opening became available at Long Island Jewish Hospital in Queens, New York. A residency spot virtually never becomes available midterm, but it did, and Murray heard of the vacancy. He immediately interviewed for the position and got it. And, off we were again to another unknown. New York City here we come!

By the time we arrived in New York, I was expecting our second child, and Gerrit was just eight months old and still breastfeeding. Much of what I knew about breastfeeding and caring for an infant, I had learned from observing the Bedouin mothers in Saudi Arabia. Thank goodness I had some real-life experiences from which to form my childcare practices, otherwise, all I had were books on parenting and childcare. Knowing that I was still breastfeeding, the obstetrician recommended I switch to bottle-feeding as soon as possible, so as not to rob nutrients from the baby I was carrying. When I, or anybody else, attempted to give Gerrit a bottle, he would fuss and cry and did not want any part of it. I didn't know what to do until I remembered the mothers in Saudi Arabia who continued to breastfeed an older child while she herself was pregnant, or even an infant and older child at the same time. I witnessed healthy babies born to these mothers, and that was very reassuring at this time. I continued to breastfeed Gerrit until we were able to wean him to the bottle, which was right before Hanneke was born. I am grateful to my Bedouin mentors.

Hanneke arrived in the Summer of 1985, and when Murray finished his residency the following July, we were off to Arizona to start the newest chapter of our then young life together. We decided that we liked living in the desert and that living in the Phoenix area afforded us easy access to the mountains and the ocean, which greatly interested us. We had finally completed what seemed like a marathon of marathons. We left the United States in November of 1981, worked as volunteers in the West Indies until the Spring of 1982, and moved to Saudi Arabia that Summer. We completed a two-year contract in Saudi Arabia and a two-year ER residency, living in both Baltimore and New York City. In just shy of five years, and two children later, we were living in Phoenix, Arizona, having completed a great deal. It was truly a whirlwind, and like a whirlwind, there was collateral damage; and in 1987, the marriage began to crumble. Our divorce was finalized in May of 1988, and as Murray walked me to my car he said, "Let's continue to do things differently like we always have." I just looked at him, but I knew it would be true. Ever since we returned to the States in 1984, we talked about someday returning to Saudi Arabia. I thought that would no longer be possible after our divorce. We were most concerned about how to manage life in the best interest of the children, and that would take time to figure out.

One day when Murray was over at the house to pick up the kids, he broached the subject of taking a job in Saudi Arabia. It was the Fall of 1989, and he had remarried earlier that year. His wife was also a doctor, and he said that they were interested in working in Saudi Arabia and wanted the kids to accompany them. Well, without thinking, I said, "If the kids go, I go." And he said, "Fine!" Well, it wasn't quite that easy, but Murray and I were pretty good at finding solutions for complex problems, not counting our marital problems. It so happened that the Canadian recruiting agency that assisted us in acquiring Murray's Saudi Arabian work visa in 1982 was still quite involved in staffing hospitals throughout Saudi Arabia. Sometime later that year, the owner of the recruitment company flew from Toronto to Phoenix to interview us separately and together, to assess whether or not we were a good risk. Apparently, it was not a normal occurrence to receive an inquiry for job openings for a married medical couple, who shared children with an ex-wife who was applying for a nursing position at the same hospital. Our interviews went well, and we were eventually offered positions., We were slated to start work at King Khalid Medical Center in Riyadh in the summer of 1990. I had applied for a pediatric nursing position and was offered a Head Nurse position, much to my delight.

The Spring and Summer of 1990 went by all too quickly, which seems to be the norm when you're uprooting your life and moving abroad. My sweet sister-in-law passed away earlier that year, which was very difficult for all of us. Making plans for a big move in the wake of such grief was not easy, but we managed. In retrospect, it's all a blur, but I do know that much time and effort went into the move. I quit my job at Phoenix Children's Hospital, rented my house to someone I knew, and sold my car. I was very committed to this move and did everything possible to make It a success. I was scheduled to fly out of Chicago the last week of July, so the kids and I flew to my stay with parents several days prior to my departure. The kids then stayed with my parents while I set off for Riyadh, and Murray and Kathy finished work and tied up loose ends in Phoenix. My parents became a strong foundation of support for Gerrit and Hanneke from that time forward.

Both sets of grandparents were extremely helpful and supportive over the years, and for that, I am very grateful.

The move really went quite smoothly, but leaving the children for the unknown was hard for the kids and for me. Gerrit was only six and Hanneke was about to turn five, and they had already had to process some difficult transitions; this was going to be a big one. My home had been our children's primary residence since we moved to Phoenix. The children spent every other weekend at Murray's after the divorce, but now his home would be their primary residence because his job afforded him Family status. When I accepted the Head Nurse position, I was told that I would have my own apartment, which would make it easy for the children to spend as much time with me as needed for them to adapt to the new living arrangement. But, before my arrival, there had been a flood of new employees and housing was at a premium, so it became necessary for me to share an apartment with another woman. Well, that is a story for another day. Suffice to say, eventually, we were able to find a solution so that the children had their own room, and we were able to make the transition as smooth as humanly possible. But, it was still hard!

## Chapter Seven
## The Gulf War
### Home and Work Life

A Week Before the Invasion of Kuwait

I was the first of our "family unit" to arrive in Riyadh in July of 1990. We thought it might be best if I started work and got settled before the others set off on their journey. Murray and his wife Kathy and the children were scheduled to leave the States a couple of weeks after my arrival. As planned, once in-country, I immediately began orientation to my new position as Head Nurse of one of the Pediatric Wards in the 500-bed Medical Center Hospital. The hospital complex was located just on the outskirts of Riyadh proper. The compound was lovely, and quite different from that of KKMC, but the process of integration was much the same. The fact that I was familiar with the language and culture was a big help. When you travel across the world, and start work the following day, jet lag is a real issue. I had a couple of mishaps due to disorientation and balance because of lack of sleep, but nothing that resulted in an injury. I ran into the plate glass window instead of the door, when exiting my apartment building that first day, and then missed the curb while crossing the street. So, instead of going exploring, I decided to go back and rest. I don't think it would have been promising if I had to take a sick day on my very first day, or worse yet, ended up in the ER before I even had a tour of the hospital. Embarrassing and funny at the same time, but true!

Eventually, I met my roommate and we established some house rules; actually, they were her house rules. She had been working at King Fahd and sharing an apartment for some time, so she seemed to know how she liked things. I didn't realize it at the time, but my roommate had a reputation for being hard to live with. Sometimes the less you know, the better it is. I filled her in on the fact that I had children, and that I hoped to have them stay with me on the weekends. Well luckily, she had a boyfriend who worked for one of the American Military Contractors, and she spent weekends with him. You can be sure I would be on the phone ASAP to discuss my situation with the Housing Supervisor. After some mindless conversation in an effort to become acquainted, I went off to bed in anticipation of the new beginning I was embarking on in the morning. Jet lag is quite the disruptor after a long flight and one's sleep is often interrupted, as was mine. Luckily, I was able to get enough sleep to get on the bus in the morning and show up at the right place for orientation. As I mentioned before, I had plenty of experience over the years as a new employee, so orientation was like going to Summer camp for me, full of adventure and new friends.

I was introduced to my new unit, and the outgoing Head Nurse laid down the ground rules of how things functioned at King Fahd Medical Center Hospital. Little did I know when I began that first week that there was a big shake-up on the horizon. Orientation wasn't too stressful so my new friend June and I thought it would be fun to go into town to see what the stores in Riyadh had to offer. We were most interested in going to the Gold Souk, or bazaar, because even if you can't afford to buy anything, it's so fun to look at all the jewelry and gawk at the prices. A shopping bus traveled into town every night, and we were determined to be on the bus right after the first evening Prayer Call so that we would have time to shop before the next Prayer call around 7:30 PM. The shops usually closed for about fifteen minutes, and then would be open until the bus returned home around 9 PM. Taking the bus into town was such a luxury, no need to drive and it didn't cost anything. What's not to like? The radio in the bus was on, and much to everyone's surprise, the music was interrupted for some "Breaking News." It's surreal to even recall what happened next. The Breaking News was that Iraq had just invaded Kuwait! The consensus at the time was that Iraq would be dealt with swiftly, and would retreat within days. I remember barely giving it a second thought. Who was Iraq anyway? Just a small country with no real power. It turns out that I knew little of the country's dictator Saddam Hussein, and the years of war between Iraq and Iran that he engaged his country in to merely demonstrate his power as a leader. We all know what happened next. I had only been in the country for a week when this occurred.

As we all know, Iraq did not retreat, and Kuwait did not have the military power to force them out. Almost immediately troops from all over the world were being deployed to Kuwait, Saudi Arabia, and the neighboring countries that were allies of Kuwait. I just kept thinking that things would get rectified soon and would go back to whatever normal was. Daily, we waited for the news that the incident was resolved, but it didn't happen. I was in Saudi Arabia in an apparently unstable situation, and my children and their dad were still back in the States. I had no idea what was going to happen. I obviously thought of going home, but we decided to wait to see if things heated up or calmed down.

The world is a more dangerous place today than it was in 1990. Or, perhaps, my optimism overshadowed the possibility of evil. It seemed that all was calm and under control, so as planned, the kids, Murray and Kathy arrived the first part of August. We, like many others, had uprooted our lives, and after months of planning were hopeful that this skirmish would blow over and life would return to normal.. For some months, it did seem that that was possible. There was a lot of watching and waiting, but nothing untoward happened.

I don't even know how to go about explaining this time in our lives. My children were living with their dad, and couldn't understand why they couldn't live with me like when we were back in the States. I would get phone calls many nights during the week, when Murray and Kathy were at work, and I would go over to help allay their fears so that they could fall asleep. They had a housekeeper, Sofie, who stayed with them when their dad and Kathy were at work, but everything was so new. School started shortly after they arrived, so to sum it up, life was a series of changes for all of us. I'm surprised we all survived the transition, especially the kids.

I have to say that most of the families and hospital workers were not worried about the situation between Iraq and Kuwait, and life was really quite "normal." I had arrived around the same time as other nurses, doctors and their families, and we all became like family. I was the only single parent on the compound, and really, over the four years I lived in Riyadh, I only met one other woman who was there with a child, and was not married. The Fall evolved in a fairly uneventful manner, except for the fact that later in the year our hospital began to make preparations in case war actually broke out. Ours was a Military hospital, so we were expected to provide support for those involved in Operation Desert Shield which became Operation Desert Storm. Life was really quite "normal." I keep using that word, but it's the only word that defines my assessment of things.

The kids went to school and made friends, and after school and on their days off they played outside, or gathered at the beautiful Recreation Center we had on the compound. On the weekends, we would go swimming or shopping. Seemingly a wonderful life, except that there was a war brewing in the region. I attended regular briefings along with other Head Nurses, Hospital Supervisors, and Hospital Administrators where the Administration updated us as to what was occurring and what we might expect. They did their best to assure us that we were in no imminent danger in Riyadh, and that our position was supportive only. When it became evident that the situation was not going to be resolved, many nurses returned to their home countries. Almost daily, when I arrived at work, another nurse or two had decided to resign, or at least take a Leave of Absence until the Gulf Crisis was resolved. Eventually, the ward I was hired to supervise closed, and I became the head nurse of another ward whose manager was on medical leave.

When I was overwhelmed by the demands of the new ward, in light of the daily changes, I would seek refuge in my patients' rooms. It was comforting to connect with my patients and their families. As the head nurse, I did not have a nursing care assignment, but there was always something needed and something I could do to help out my nurses. The rooms housed two, three or four patients and their mothers. Very often quite a conversation would ensue between the mothers, myself, and the nurses responsible for the care of that particular room. I constantly learned something new about life in Saudi Arabia, the traditions and customs, and what was most important to those I encountered at this unprecedented time in the country's history. It was a good way to focus on something other than the frightening unknown.

This is a good time to introduce my friend Salwa. Salwa was a physician I worked with on the Pediatric ward at King

Fahd for much of my four years there. She was originally from Egypt, and her husband, who was also a doctor, was originally from Jordan. They apparently met in Chicago years earlier while they were both residents, she in Pediatrics and he in Surgery. Salwa and her husband arrived in Riyadh with their youngest child many years before I did. They were quite well established in their medical practices in the States, but understood the benefit of working and living in Saudi Arabia, as did most of us who chose to relocate there. Since I had been in Saudi Arabia before, I felt somewhat familiar with the multinational team, and quite comfortable engaging in conversation.

During the workday, we often spent time talking amongst the doctors and other members of the health care team in our break room or in the nurse's station. Soon after the invasion of Kuwait, I remember Salwa and another doctor who was the Head of Pediatrics and a couple of the floor nurses and I talking about the situation. I made some assertions about what I thought of the whole situation, not really knowing much about it except what I had recently read or heard. In recalling the incident, I couldn't even tell you what I said, but the words no sooner left my lips and Salwa said," What do you know about life in the Middle East? Have you ever gone months without being able to leave your home like the Palestinians on the West Bank?" "Or been without running water or electricity for years because of unrest?" I didn't know what to say. I didn't even know what she spoke of. I knew of the difficulties in the region, but had no personal experience. Right or wrong, I have been pretty cautious about making assumptions or forming opinions from limited information I have heard or read, and became determined to research more thoroughly important topics.

Since that time, I am much more careful when I engage in conversation about complex issues. I endeavor to speak about what I do know, not because I don't want to be told off, but out of respect for those whose lives I speak of and who are most affected. Salwa and I discussed many complex issues over the years, and I learned a lot about Egypt from her relating her experience growing up there. It was quite interesting to find out that she also lived in Skokie, a suburb of Chicago. She shared that in her neighborhood various Holidays were celebrated throughout the year, some houses decorated Christmas trees and hung Christmas lights, others lit a Menorah in the window, and yet another celebrated Diwali, the Hindu festival of lights. She brought up the diversity in her neighborhood to demonstrate how people of various religions can live in harmony.

You might have thought that that encounter would have soured our relationship, but it didn't. I think it allowed us to be candid with each other from the start. I knew that Salwa would be open and honest with me, and she eventually knew that she could expect the same from me. The well-being of our patients depended on our ability to work as a team and have complete trust in each other's word. I can't recount many of the specific experiences we had, but we worked together for a good part of the four years that I was at King Fahd caring for many fragile patients. It's my recollection that she and her husband decided to leave during the final year of my contract. It was sad to see her go, both professionally and personally. I spent a time or two over a cup of tea at her lovely villa, discussing our families and her experience in Chicago prior to coming to Saudi Arabia. Our relationship was complex at times, somewhat because of our different upbringings and culture, but professionally we always seemed to find common ground.

By Christmas of 1990 things were starting to look a little uncertain in regards to peace between Iraq and Kuwait. We had remained hopeful that things would calm down and an agreement would be reached to avert war, but that didn't appear to be the case. Right after Christmas, Murray flew to Edmonton with the kids, where they would remain until a peaceful solution was attained in the region. About the same time I flew home to the States, first to Phoenix to visit friends and check on my house, and then to visit my parents in Wisconsin. Unfortunately, my father had fallen ill, and was hospitalized a good distance from my parent's hometown. I spent days visiting him in the hospital, and providing much needed moral support for my mother. After several days in Wisconsin, I was off to be with Gerrit and Hanneke in Canada before my return to Riyadh. It was while I was there that allied air forces began air and missile attacks on military targets in Iraq and Kuwait because Iraqi forces refused to retreat. That was January 17th, 1990.

I remained in Canada for another week or so, until the Riyadh airport reopened to commercial flights. The children were enrolled in school, riding the bus and playing in the snow when they were home from school. Except for visiting their other grandparents in Wisconsin at Christmastime, they had never worn snowsuits before. A fond memory was watching them on a sled with their 70 something grandpa sliding down a big hill at the park. For the nine weeks they were in Canada, snowsuits were a big part of life on the frozen prairie. Obviously, this was not an easy time, but the time with the kids was precious to the grandparents.

I returned to Riyadh the last week of January 1991, and on returning to work, I was fitted with a gas mask. I was instructed to take my gas mask with me at all times, and to put it on whenever I heard the scud missile warning siren. I was grateful to have my own gas mask because the supply was limited, but it was really difficult to get on. Thankfully, there were never any warnings that occurred in the daytime during my work hours. Prior to the beginning of the actual war, we were told multiple times by the Military that there was only a one in one million chance of a scud ever reaching Riyadh. However, scuds did reach Riyadh. Eighteen scuds were fired at Riyadh between January 21st and February 24th, 1991, thankfully without casualties in Riyadh. Most of the scud activity was late at night or early morning. Initially, when I heard the scud siren I took out the gas mask, and put it on until the All-Clear was called. There were only five or six days scud alert sirens in Riyadh after my return. I have to admit that after the first couple of times, I just didn't bother with the gas mask. It seemed that if a scud hit, by the time I got the mask on it would be too late to be of any benefit. In retrospect, I think my whole understanding of what benefit it was to afford was flawed. It was my understanding that the gas masks we were issued were used in WWII, newer equipment was being used by the soldiers. Regardless, it was a gas mask.

One night rather soon after being issued my gas mask, I went into town to visit a friend. It was only when I got ready to go home that I realized I didn't have my mask. I had left it in the taxi, failing to take it with me when I got out of the taxi. I didn't have a regular driver at that time, so I didn't even know my driver's name. I called Security on my return home, and amazingly, the taxi cab driver had already turned it into Security. The carrier had a tag with my name on it inside, so they knew the it belonged to me. There was limited supply of gas masks, so it was probable that I would not be issued another one if it was lost. It's important to note that the driver had not been issued a gas mask, and he returned mine into Security anyway. I thought that was incredible.

February 1991 was surreal. I cannot describe it any other way. At that time, I was a pediatric nurse, and it had been years since I cared for adults in the hospital. To better serve casualties of Operation Desert Storm, certain pediatric admissions were routed to other hospitals, and my ward was designated the Psychiatric Unit. I don't think we had a Psychiatrist in our hospital, but one may have been assigned from the military support unit that arrived. I was always interested in mental health, but this assignment was a bit of a surprise and caused me some sleepless nights. Thankfully, once Operation Desert Shield became Desert Storm, we started to receive medically trained support personnel. Of the nurses I received, one was a Major in the Army who was an experienced

Psychiatric Nurse, and another was a Captain who worked in Psychiatry.

With the assistance of the Psychiatric nurses, I developed Stress Management material to help staff maneuver through this time. Because the war was brief, and we saw limited casualties, our floor admitted only a handful of patients over the two-month period. Our classes were fairly well attended while the war was on, but as soon as it was over, that was the end of it. I guess nobody was stressed anymore. I was definitely appreciative of this material. They say you teach what you need to learn. During that time, I spent a great deal of time providing my military colleagues information about Saudi Arabian culture and customs, and some essential words and phrases in Arabic. I was grateful to have had prior experience in the Kingdom.

I hate to admit that this time was actually exciting and somewhat fun, in a weird way. The military personnel were visitors, and working with them was interesting and out of the ordinary. I learned a great deal about Psychiatric Nursing in the two month period that the military nurses worked with us on our ward. The nurses assigned to work with us were all too happy to share whatever information would help us prepare for any admissions we would receive. I was honored to share my knowledge about life in Saudi Arabia, as well as what I knew of the citizens, customs and language of the country.

Our compound restaurant was always pretty popular, but during this time, it was busier than ever. When we were all around the tables laughing and having fun, it seemed like being in an episode of MASH. As I said earlier, we never received many casualties in our hospital, so the overall stress surrounding the situation was low for most employees. Much of the stress was a result of the media experts predicting gloom and doom, causing family members back home to call and plead their loved one's to return. I remember hearing stories on TV when I was back home that didn't seem to correlate to our lives in Riyadh. Pretty frustrating.

The month of February was coming to its end, and there was talk of a resolution on the horizon. Never being in this situation before, it was hard to know what to believe. I continued to conduct my personal and work life as usual, by going to work and performing my work well, and then returning home to relax and rejuvenate for the next day. It was after supper on February 24th, 1991, when the scud siren sounded. I was in my apartment, sitting on my bed talking to a friend on the phone. Moments later, the cherished words, "All Clear!" sounded. Those two words were music to my ears. After all was clear, I told my friend that the next time the siren sounds, I was going to go outside, thinking it would be safer than remaining in the four-story apartment I lived in. Thankfully, that was the last scud fired at Riyadh, and the last "All-Clear" called. On February 28th 1991, Operation Desert Storm ended. The military support personnel remained at the hospital for a short time, making certain that the truce was lasting. Middle East experts felt certain that it would be best for Sadaam Hussain to remain in power because of the many unstable groups in the region. We all waited to see how things transpired, and for the most part, it seemed that everything calmed down and we pretty much went back to life as usual.

March came, the kids returned home to Riyadh and I resumed my position as Head Nurse on the Pediatric ward I was previously assigned. Slowly, many of the nurses who left during Operation Desert Storm returned and we resumed our work, although many of us would really never be the same. Life became what you might call normal, even new nurses and Medical Staff arrived from all parts of the world, which boosted our capability to better care for patients. I guess returning to a region that was once considered within the field of operation during wartime is much like flying on a company's airplane right after one had crashed the day before; not likely to happen again anytime soon. But, I had decided to return once war broke out, so those of us attracted to this kind of work/life opportunity seem to march to the beat of a different drum, or in this case the same drum. Throughout this whole time, the majority of Saudi Nationals I encountered, and with whom I worked, were very thankful for my service, and the support of the United States. Of course, there were always the exceptions.

Most of my interactions and stories are of a positive nature, and that's what prompted me to write this book, because my experiences were by and large good. To be fair, I need to share a couple of instances that happened right around the time of the Gulf War, either during or immediately after it ended and the majority of troops went home. The first occurrence happened one night when I was shopping in one of the popular outdoor malls. It was in the evening and I was just walking down the sidewalk. I think I was alone, but am not completely certain. The other instance occurred at work between myself and a Social Worker. It was odd in that I needed a Social Worker to handle a delicate matter, and the person who arrived to assist me I had never met before. I believe the situation took place on the weekend, and the Social Worker on call generally worked on an adult ward. The following is what I remember of the interactions.

Women were expected to wear an abaya over their attire when out in public, but not on our compound. A head cover was suggested, but not all ExPatriot women followed this suggestion. For the most part, if you wore an abaya, the Mutawa, or religious police, would be satisfied. I had gone into town to shop one evening, and was about to cross the street when a Mutawa approached me and asked why I wore a "too-short" abaya. Well, that was a good question. I was a bit of a cheapskate and was happy to be the recipient of a hand-me-down abaya when I first arrived in Riyadh. The abaya was very short, about calf length, which was shorter than the recommended ankle length. In addition, I tied the abaya around the collar region, instead of pinning it, which caused it to hike up in the middle, making it even shorter.

The Mutawa addressed me in English, with what seemed to be an American accent, so I responded in English. I didn't have an excuse for my abaya's length, but I told him that I didn't realize it was considered too short. Then we seemed to get into a disagreement. He went on to say that I was disrespectful of Saudi Arabian customs, like many Americans. I answered that I was not disrespectful, telling him that I was a nurse who cared for children in the hospital, and that I remained in Saudi Arabia during the war because I cared about its citizens. He replied that the only reason myself, and those like me, work in Saudi Arabia, is to make more money than we could at home. That wasn't completely true, but he did have a point. I decided to stop bantering with him. He then told me to cover my head, but I didn't have a scarf. He threatened that if he saw me later that night without a head cover, he would arrest me. I voiced understanding. I decided to take a taxi home and not risk running into him again. I'm not certain I ever did get the headscarf.

When I returned to work the next day, I shared my story with our Pediatric Nephrology resident. He shared that his wife never covered her head when shopping, but that she only shopped in certain more upscale shopping areas where the Mutawa didn't bother women about headscarves. Who knew that this was even possible? Many of my Saudi friends encouraged me not to cover, and to frequent less conservative areas in Riyadh. One friend said, "If you cover your face, then the Mutawa want you to wear gloves, if you wear gloves, then they want you to stay in the car, if you're sitting in a parked car, they recommend you to go home" Interesting! So, I purchased a longer abaya, but rarely wore a head scarf unless I decided to shop in a more conservative region of Riyadh. Many of my friends told me that covering was really for Muslims, and not so much to be reinforced if you were non-Muslim. It was also recommended to avoid engaging in conversation, especially in disagreement, with a Mutawa. Good advice!

Shortly after the Gulf War ended, I had an unfavorable run-in with a male Social Worker in our hospital. I was on duty one weekend, and required the expertise of a Social Worker, but all who normally covered Pediatrics were off that day. I asked the Operator to page the Social Worker on-call, and a man I had not met before answered my page and later arrived on the floor.

I can't remember how we got into such an unpleasant interaction, but at some point in our conversation he seemed compelled to tell me that he was not happy about the American Military being in Riyadh during Operation Desert Shield and Desert Storm. He further said that the American influence, women in the military driving vehicles, and disregard for Islamic rules, was bad for Saudi Arabia. He seemed to feel that the bad outweighed the good in regards to what the United States contributed to the country.

I was pretty much speechless throughout his rant; but I did say that I was sorry he felt that way, and that I had never heard this sentiment expressed by any other Saudi Arabian citizen I had communicated with over these past several months. He went on to say that his children didn't like Americans either. Well, I got the information I needed and terminated our conversation. I immediately reported the incident to my supervisor, as well as this man's supervisor. This man and many like him, like Osama Bin Laden, when he was still living in Saudi Arabia, were fearful of what might happen if the citizens of Saudi Arabia desired a freer society. Today, I know this man was not alone in the feelings he shared with me that day in 1991. I never saw him again, and never again did I ever run across an individual with such feelings, from that time until I returned home in 1994. Thank goodness!

The kids and I went home to the States on vacation during the summer of 1991, and by all accounts, things appeared to be back to normal. By the time Thanksgiving and Christmas rolled around, memories of the war seemed to truly be a thing of the past.

The various Embassies were always hosting Holiday Galas at this time of year, and this year the Canadian Embassy organized a Holiday/Christmas Celebration in the desert just outside of Riyadh. Marriott catered the event and there was singing and games for the children. Bleachers were set up for the families to observe the happenings and listen to the children singing Christmas Carols. As they started to sing "Here Comes Santa Claus," over the nearest crest came Santa Claus on a camel. The children were off to greet him as if they had all been shot out of a cannon. Parents were asked to purchase a gift of a certain value for their child(ren) for Santa to present to them. The day's event was magical and I have never forgotten the joy and laughter! We were truly a family of Nations that day. Thank you, Canada!

Christmas was always a special time while living in Saudi Arabia. In the early years and even in 1990, receiving a Christmas greeting from colleagues from Muslim countries, including Saudi Arabia, was quite common. The following years, the greeting was generally "Happy Holiday!" Early on, if you wanted to decorate for Christmas, you pretty much had to bring decorations from home. In 1990, I received a hand-me-down pre-decorated white artificial Christmas tree with a few other festive items, including well preserved used Christmas wrapping paper. During the Christmas Season of 1993, Christmas lights, bulbs, and wrapping paper were readily available in many stores in Riyadh. I actually felt a little let down. For some reason reusing the paper and decorating with items that had been accumulated over the years seemed to make it more special in an odd way. Once you could purchase all the decorations you wanted at the store made it seem more commonplace to me. It's hard to explain. I do think, however, it was cool that Christmas was readily acknowledged by many, which was also very special.

One of the fondest memories I have of Christmas, outside of the fabulous Canadian Christmas of 1991, was our first Christmas in Saudi Arabia in 1982. We made a turkey dinner and invited most of our friends for dinner and dancing on Christmas Eve. While I was waiting for the company to arrive, I went outside on our back patio for some reason. Although it was not a full moon, it was quite bright and Venus was very visible in the sky just after dusk. Off in the distance on the other side of the compound fence, sat a Bedouin gentleman on his donkey. It was really quite unreal because it was Christmas Eve and I had never seen this man and his donkey before or since. I went in to get Murray and by the time we returned he was gone. I took it as a sign from above. We were celebrating Christmas in a Muslim country and did not have any of the usual decorations and were far from away from our families. But, I believe I received a real-life depiction of that

First Christmas in this gentleman on his donkey, and it made my Christmas extra special.

Chapter Eight
# LIFE AFTER DESERT STORM
Coworkers, Patients and Friends

I worked with Abdulaziz for most of the four years I was in Riyadh. He had worked as a ward clerk at King Fahd for years before I arrived on the scene. It didn't take me very long to figure out that he had an attendance problem that was well known by everyone, but there seemed to be little recourse. It was very difficult to terminate a Saudi National unless there were serious grounds, such as getting into a fight with a patient or coming to work intoxicated, which would never be the case with Abdulaziz. It became clear that I would have to develop some way to encourage Abdulaziz to be the employee our ward needed. He was married and unfortunately had quite sickly children, which often caused him to be late to work or not show at all. There was usually an excuse, but not a good one according to Western standards. There was no excuse for not calling, but for some reason I chose to focus on his positive attributes, and get more from him when he was at work. I saw him as an extremely capable and emotionally intelligent human being. When he was at work, his accomplishments were unequaled in his ability to interpret necessary medical information and obtain consents for procedures, and to help us gain the trust of our patients and their families. I truly felt that he helped me a great deal in relating to patients, which allowed me to be much more effective.

I found out later that Abdulaziz also was responsible for his mother. She had been married and divorced, and then married and widowed, and was on her own. So, he had a lot on his plate, as they say. Women could not drive in Saudi Arabia at that time in history, so if Abdulaziz needed to get his family to appointments or assist with his mother's needs, he was the designated driver. The older I am, I realize that not everyone handles the demands of family life in the same way, and Abdulaziz had a difficult time planning ahead and managing his work responsibilities in addition to that of his home life. In my eyes, he made up for the attendance issue in the effort he put into the work he did when at the hospital. We had many conversations of family and faith over the years, and I considered him a good and ethical man.

My favorite memory in thinking of my relationship with Abdulaziz was the time he had decided he wanted to transfer to the department of Patient Relations. He asked me if I would write a Letter of Recommendation for him. "Of course," I told him. I could easily write a letter of recommendation, highlighting his many attributes, complementary of him as a person, and the quality of his work. But then, he asked that I not mention his tardiness or absenteeism. I told Abdulaziz that I couldn't lie, I'd have to be truthful if he wanted me to write a letter for him. In explaining why this was necessary in my mind, I gave him an example, hoping he would understand. I said, "Abdulaziz, what if I don't tell the truth about your attendance, and you get the job, and it's not right for you after all? However, if I tell the truth, and leave the results to God, then things will turn out as they should. If you get the job or don't get the job, it'll be the best for you." Abdulaziz understood and agreed, and he got the job.

Abdulaziz transferred to his new job before I left Riyadh. As I waited for the limo to take me to the airport one last time, Abdulaziz came running into the hospital with a gift for me. One last time, Abdulaziz was later than expected, but as usual, his gift of the 24-karat gold rimmed Austrian crystal glasses and his heartfelt farewell did not disappoint. That was Abdulaziz!

My first real love in nursing was nephrology, and taking care of patients with chronic kidney disease. It just so happened that in my hospital in Riyadh, pediatric patients with kidney conditions were assigned to my unit. The Nephrologist that worked in our hospital was a very dedicated doctor, and interested in developing needed programs that did not yet exist for our patients. He was always writing journal articles and compiling research to advance the practice of Pediatric Nephrology and ultimately the lives of our patients.

With our doctor's assistance, we developed a home dialysis program for patients whose parents wanted to learn and had an acceptable home environment. Our program taught patients and their families how to safely perform dialysis in the home, allowing them to have a more normal life. The procedure was performed at various hours throughout the day, gave the patient and the family free time, keeping them from having to go to a unit outside of the home three to four days during the week.

I was blessed with a very competent and knowledgeable nursing staff, but it became evident that a natural Arabic speaker and a nurse devoted to our Home Dialysis Program alone was needed. We advertised the position in Riyadh, and eventually hired an nurse who lived in Riyadh with her family, and was educated and licensed as a nurse in the United States. She was perfect for the job, having lived many years in the Middle East. Coupled with knowledge of the Arabic language and its culture, she was a wonderful asset and essential piece of our dialysis program's puzzle.

We became good friends, and I enjoyed our times together. If my memory is correct, her mother was from the States and her father from Iraq. Stories she shared of her childhood were so special to me, especially on the backdrop of the Gulf War. It was wonderful to have real life examples of people living in Iraq, not only those in the news. Her children were close in age to my children, so we socialized from time to time as a family. One year Shareen invited us to dinner on Christmas Eve, and she seemed to go out of her way to prepare a truly traditional American Christmas dinner. Her mother was from the Midwest, so many of the specialties she served that night were similar to those of Christmases I remembered. We so enjoyed ourselves that night, it was the highlight of my Holiday Season.

Shareen worked at King Fahd for about a year when her husband received a job offer he accepted in Jeddah. In no time, we were invited to their new home, which we readily accepted. We had never been to Jeddah before, and it was a real treat. Walking on the boardwalk along the coast of the Red Sea was magical. But, my favorite memory is the early morning Prayer Call sounding through the open window of the room where I was sleeping. It was an annoyance on one hand, and quite magnificent on the other. The Prayer Call that morning was sung, and was quite lovely. Unfortunately, it awakened my young children, and the chance of sleeping in on my day off was not going to happen. Visiting Shareen and her family was like visiting family; times I have always cherished.

The kids were invited to visit during Spring Break that year. Murray and I were in agreement that the trip would be a nice experience for the kids, and we had complete confidence they would be in good hands. I walked Gerrit and Hanneke to the gate where the airplane was waiting, and a flight attendant escorted them to their seats. They were excited to go to Jeddah, so our goodbyes was short and sweet. Shareen, her husband and their kids met them once they arrived in Jeddah.

Gerrit and Hanneke returned home with many stories of their visit. Shareen's home was a interesting mix of Western and Middle Eastern culture and customs, and my kids seem to enjoy the variety. Very shortly after their visit, Shareen informed me that her husband was taking a job in the States, and they would be leaving Saudi Arabia. I was sad about the news as it affected me, but that's the ExPat life. We stayed in touch for years, but due to my moving and new phone numbers, we lost touch. Just recently we were able to find each other online, and it was wonderful to reminisce about our time together in Riyadh.

Mohammed was what you might call a "regular" or "frequent flyer" on our ward. He and his mother spent many weeks at a time in our hospital because had been diagnosed with End-Stage Kidney Disease, and he needed dialysis. He was only six years old, and was quite small for his age. Because he and his mother spent so much time in the hospital and were so easy to get along with, we seemed to develop a close bond over time. I was generally very fond of my patients. There's always one or two that are difficult to connect with, but that was an exception. Mohammed had Chronic Kidney Disease and he required dialysis. Mohammed was actually the impetus for our unit to develop the CAPD Program.

With the assistance of our Nephrologist, Shareen and my many talented nurses, Mohammed was able to go home and stay home unless he ran into problems. The advent of this program allowed this little boy to live at home with his parents and little sister. Our criteria for allowing a patient to be discharged on home dialysis was quite strict. We screened the parents as to their ability to follow the instructions for care, a demonstration of the procedure prior to discharge and the condition of the home. The home had to be clean to decrease the risk of infection. Prior to discharge, I made a home visit to make sure the environment was suitable for the procedure to be performed safely. Mohammed's mother passed the test with flying colors.

Mohammed's father was a Mutawah, which meant that he was a member of what was called the "religious police," or a designation for those who enforced the religious rules throughout the neighborhoods they lived in or were assigned to. I guess that Mohammed's father was so grateful for the care we provided his little boy that he extended courtesies that you wouldn't expect of a Mutawah. When he visited Mohammed, he always greeted me politely, looked me in the eye when he spoke, and generally shook my hand in greeting. That behavior was very unusual and unexpected. Mohammed's mother was a warm and loving woman, and I was able to relate to her easily. My children were close in age to Mohammed, so we used to share stories when I would make my patient rounds throughout the day. When I visited Mohammed at his home, prior to beginning home dialysis, his mother and father welcomed me warmly.

Mohammed's mother had recently had a baby, and I was able to meet the new little one. We shared a cup a tea, and

I was soon off. While visiting, I found out that Mohammed's father had another wife. Mohammed's mother was his second wife, and wife #1 lived in another part of Riyadh. Mohammed's mother spoke of her in a positive manner and from all accounts everything was quite amicable. Mohammed's father seemed like a gentle and kind man who treated his children and his wife with apparent affection.

There was a difference in how Mohammed's father interacted with me when I was in their home. He did not make eye contact with me when we spoke and there was no shaking hands on greeting. I guess there was a different code of ethics for when he was in a Western Hospital and I was the person in charge. I don't know that, it's just an observation and my speculation. One day nearing the time I would be leaving to return to the States, Mohammed and his parents visited me at the hospital. Mohammed and his family were themselves getting ready to go to the States. Apparently there were no Kidney Transplant doctors in Saudi Arabia who felt comfortable performing a kidney transplant on Mohammed because of his size. He had received word from the doctor in the U.S.

that if he could come to the States, he would be placed on the Kidney Transplant list, and then there would be a good chance he might get a kidney. So, they went to the United States in search of a kidney, and I did hear that Mohammed was fortunate to receive one. When he was about to leave for the United States, his family gave me a watch with the Map of Riyadh on it. I wore that watch almost daily until I wore it out. I cherish the fact that we cared for and had such respect for each other. What a gift.

I really didn't play favorites on the floor, but it was hard to not become fond of a patient who had a lovely soul, and was hospitalized for weeks at a time. Gazwah and I bonded in a special way. It was not a bonding that afforded her any special perks as a patient, but just being in her presence made my heart sing. For some reason, regardless of our different backgrounds, I was able to understand her fears and her needs as a chronically ill 14 year old, which helped her navigate the many hospitalizations she required because of her condition. At this point in my nursing career, I had been a pediatric nurse for about 8 years, and my primary nursing experience had been on acute

Pediatric Medical/Surgical wards. My absolute favorite nursing specialty was Pediatric Nephrology, and for some reason adolescents. I guess I felt generally misunderstood as an adolescent, so I tried my best to understand the needs of this particular patient population.

Gazwah had Chronic Kidney Disease and needed to start dialysis. When she underwent surgery for the insertion of a peritoneal dialysis access tubing, I was able to be at her side and talk her through her post-operative time when her parents weren't able to be there because of other family demands. My love and understanding of Pediatric Nephrology, as well as her ability to understand my Arabic, was invaluable. Because I had a basic command of the Arabic language spoken by many of our Saudi National patients, Gazwah seemed comfortable to ask me questions and confide in me when afraid.

I became very well acquainted with her family, especially her mother and father. In fact, when making home visits with a Social Worker to the homes of some of our chronic long-term patients, I was welcomed into Gazwah's home like a relative or friend. It just so happened that her older sister had just delivered a baby, and she and her newborn returned to her parents' home, as is customary in Saudi Arabia after a woman delivers a baby. I was told that the mother and baby receive the support of the grandmother and other family members for about six weeks. The mother is given the time to recover from childbirth and regain her strength. After the six weeks, she then returns home better able to provide for her baby, while resuming her duties in the home. I was amazed to hear of this tradition, but learned later on that this is a common practice in many cultures.

Gazwah eventually received a kidney transplant, and after she recovered on the transplant unit, she returned to our floor to complete her recovery prior to discharge home. One time her father and her mother and a few siblings, as well as her father's second wife, came to the hospital to visit. I was invited to join the "family" as they congregated on the hospital grounds on a couple of big blankets. We shared cups of tea and biscuits as we bantered back and forth. I mostly just listened and laughed. Gazwa's father's second wife lived on the second floor of the villa her family lived in. Everybody got along well. I initially thought that the other lady with the family that day was Gazwa's aunt. Well, she could have been. Relations were very friendly. But, I think that was the general atmosphere in their house. Gazwa's father was a very kind and gentle man. Caring for Gazwah and interacting with her family was one of the bright spots of my time at King Fahd. Gazwah and Mohammed had exceptional family situations as far as I could see. And, it was a pleasure to share my life with them.

There are so many different stories of parties and events that occurred over the four years I worked and lived in Riyadh. Two people that constantly come to mind are my ward clerks, Amani and Wafa. Amani was from Egypt and Wafa originally from Yemen. They were both lovely, kind and gentle women. Amani was married and had children, and seemed a natural beauty. Wafa was much younger and unmarried, never wore makeup at work and displayed a quiet simplicity. One night Wafa came to a party dressed in couture, wearing makeup, and a fashionable hairdo. She looked like a Supermodel! We were all blown away! I would never have even guessed that Wafa was interested in fashion or the such. As they say, never judge a book by its cover.

We worked together, shared stories of our families, our backgrounds, and our dreams during the lulls of a day's work. My staff loved to celebrate birthdays and throw parties for any occasion. I held "girl" parties at my apartment and attended those hosted at other flats many times over the years. It was what we did. The women who attended these parties were from countries all over the world. Girls parties always had a form of belly dancing, without the belly exposed, and a sash over the clothes. It was so much fun! Eating, dancing, singing and laughing is common to most cultures and translates easily!

I had only been at work for a few weeks when a ward clerk from another ward invited me to dinner with other nurses she knew well. I thought that dress would be quite conservative, so I didn't really have anything terribly fancy or flashy to wear. Our hostess was the daughter of a Captain in one of the branches of the Military, and lived in another part of town. She and her driver picked us up and drove us to her family's villa. At first glance, even covered, she appeared quite glamorous. When we got to her home and we all took off our abayas, she was dressed in French couture and I looked like a country bumpkin. I was to find out that this was going to be a common thread when we were invited for dinner at the homes of our Saudi Arabian friends. The women always dressed very fashionably and in a very sexy manner. Don't let the cover fool you.

Early on I found out that when you are invited to someone's home for dinner, especially if you are invited to a wedding reception, you need to eat before you leave home. You will not be eating until late! I went to a wedding once and dinner was not served until midnight. Lots of talking, dancing and laughing, Saudi champagne, which is apple juice and sparkling water, and hard candy covered almonds. Don't get me wrong, I had fun, but if you don't eat beforehand, or take a nap before you go, the night gets really long. Overtime, I figured out the best time to arrive and then asked my driver to return at a specific time. It's pretty much like in the States, if you're not part of the wedding party or a relative, you can make a quiet exit without anyone noticing. It's hard to turn down an invitation to a party or wedding; it's all in the strategic planning.

From time to time, my children accompanied me to parties at some of my coworkers' villas off compound. I loved for my kids to experience the culture and the food. I remember a time when Gerrit and Hanneke joined me, and Amani's children were at the party. The kids spent the whole time riding bikes and playing on the roof of the villa. I remember when they came down to join us and saw all the women dancing, Gerrit's eyes widened as he took in the sight. This was a much different atmosphere than parties hosted by our American and Canadian friends. No alcohol, but a great deal of laughing and dancing!

I could go on and on about these times. Many Saudi female residents and other coworkers and colleagues were very gracious and generous. If you were invited to someone's villa, it was certain you would be treated like royalty. I have nothing but fond memories of my visits to the home's of these women, from the time we were picked up by their driver, to meeting their family and then the dinner and fun that followed. These times together seemed to strengthen our bond at work. We truly were like a family. But, don't get me wrong, there were times when tough conversations were necessary, and we seemed to weather those times with respect.

One such time I recall involved three nurses from Alexandria, Egypt. All three were friends and had known each other for some time. Two of the nurses were very strong in their knowledge and their skills, and the other somewhat weak, so required a fair bit of my attention after the standard orientation. Eventually, they were all on their own, and were often on different days and shifts. Over time, I started to notice that there was frostiness between the two. I had a really good rapport with the two nurses that I described as stronger. It wasn't because of their nursing abilities, they just seemed easier to relate to and communicate with. For some reason, the other was a bit aloof and more difficult to engage with.

One day, one of the nurses with whom I had a good rapport came to me crying, saying that she couldn't work with the other anymore. I asked her to tell me what had happened, and why she felt that way. It seemed that she and the nurse I described as being aloof had a falling out regarding a personal matter. It was a situation that seemed to hurt her at a very deep level. What was I to do? When you are in charge of making the schedule for a nursing ward, having to consider vacations, patient needs, nurse's strengths and weaknesses, you certainly can't be bothered if nurses can't get along. That would be a nightmare! I knew that these women were practicing Muslims, and took their faith seriously.

I spoke to each one of the nurses individually, and about friendship, and how problems arise when working and living together. Then we talked about our walk with God, and what our commitment to Him is in our thoughts and actions. Like my conversation with Abdulaziz, I would never have a conversation like this at work in the United States. But, it was the perfect approach for this issue, as we had all discussed our individual beliefs in the past. Thankfully, the problem was eventually resolved in a respectful manner, and the two nurses were able to work on my unit. I'm not certain their relationship was ever completely repaired, but the two women were able to work together as professionals.

CHAPTER NINE
# TURKISH HOSPITALITY
ISTAMBUL, ISMIR AND KUSADASI

My friend Fatma and I stayed connected over the years through letters and phone calls since saying our goodbyes in 1984. One day I received a letter from her, telling me that she had met and married a Turkish man, one who had studied in the United States and returned to Turkey to start a business. All the years I had known Fatma, there was one thing for certain, she would never marry a traditional Turkish male. Well, leave it to Fatma, she somehow met a man who studied abroad and returned to Turkey with "an open mind." Before I knew it, I received another letter with a photo of their baby girl "Rosebud." Rosebud was the Western meaning of her Turkish name. The name made perfect sense to me because Fatma was very proud of the fact that Turkish rose oil was famous for its excellent quality, and was highly sought after in the French perfume industry.

When I returned to Saudi Arabia, my children and I traveled to Turkey in the Winter of 1991. Fatma and her husband Cenk invited us to visit them at their home in the beautiful seaside village of Kusadasi. Cenk owned a travel agency, and he and Fatma planned our whole trip for us. On arrival, there was a driver waiting for us, and he took us to our hotel. The kids and I wandered around Istanbul for a few days, and then set off on a bus trip they had arranged for us to take to Izmir and then on to Kusadasi. When we arrived in Kusadasi, Fatma and her husband picked us up at the bus depot, and soon after we went out to dinner at a traditional Turkish restaurant in their hometown. It was such a fun time.

When we returned home from dinner, Fatma explained that she would have to leave in the morning for Istanbul to be admitted for back surgery. Turkey has a form of socialized medicine, and she had been on a waitlist to have the surgery for some months. She explained that a date opened up on her surgeon's schedule, and she needed to take it or lose her spot, and begin the whole process over.

She obviously had to go, but certainly, we would have to find another place to stay? Fatma insisted that we stay with her family. We had just met her husband and their little girl. It just didn't seem right. But, Cenk's niece was also living with them, and she assured me that they wanted us to stay. So, we remained as house guests for the week, as we had planned. It was a bit strange, but Cenk and his niece made us feel very welcomed and comfortable.

It just so happened that when we were in Turkey, the country saw its first snowfall in years, and was naturally much colder than usual for that time of year. And, added to that, Fatma's solar unit wasn't working, and there was no heat. There was a wood-burning stove in the living room, which was where my children and Rosebud slept since it was the warmest part of the house. Cenk stayed with the children, so I didn't have to worry about them being cold. I slept in a bedroom with no heat, but the blankets were wool, so unless I decided to venture outside of the covers, all was well.

Fatma was very apologetic, but what could she do? Not only was there no heat in the bedroom where I slept, there was none in the bathroom, either. As I recall, there were a few solar units or panels, and the one that was not working controlled the furnace and water heater. I seem to remember that we had lights, and the television worked. I had to use cold water to wash myself in what was an already cold room. I didn't want to appear to be a wimp, so I tried to wash up as much as possible without asking for water to be heated on the stove. Needless to say, I wasn't the cleanest tourist in Kusadasi that week in December. Thank goodness I grew up spending a great deal of time roughing it when I visited my Great Aunt Anne. She lived in the country, and had to pump her own water, and seldom used the generator for power. So, I was quite accustomed to washing up in the sink and using an outhouse. That week really wasn't so bad, just a minor inconvenience, and makes for a good story. I managed to take the whole thing in stride and to be quite honest, it didn't seem to affect my children in the least.

The area where we stayed was somewhat rural with wide-open fields and olive groves interwoven. The kids would go out exploring while I got myself ready to go into town. One day they came running home all out of breath and told me that they had been chased by a bull. What on earth! Oh my goodness! I guess you never know what you're in for when you're in unfamiliar territory. I had scoped out the area before allowing them to venture out, but a bull being in the vicinity just wasn't on my radar. I had always been so overprotective of my children, I found it funny that I felt secure letting them go out on their own. Fortunately, this was a wake-up call, and no one got hurt. This episode reminds me of the time my family visited my uncle and his family in California. I was about 11 years old at the time, and we were staying at a cabin in Yosemite National Park. The grown-ups were making dinner, and we kids decided to go exploring. We all set out in groups of two, and whatever the objective was I can't remember. Well, we happened to spot a deer and set out after it. Before we knew it we were incredibly lost. I didn't think I would ever see my parents again. Thankfully, we were able to trace our steps back to the cabin. To this day, I have no idea how we managed that. In remembering that feeling, I made sure my kids were within my field of vision from that time on, until we returned home.

On another memorable day, we ventured into the town of Kusadasi to see what we could see. I wanted to go to a Turkish restaurant and experience the local cuisine, but my children were in the mood for something familiar. So, we went to a Turkish Pizza place, featuring wood-fired pizza. In 1992, wood-fired pizza was quite uncommon in the States, I had never seen a pizza oven before, and it was a fun experience for all of us. We walked the streets and when we became hungry on another day, we found a place where we could get a type of panini. I had never had a panini before, so lots of firsts. One of my fondest memories is when we walked around Kusadasi one afternoon and saw men pushing wheelbarrows full of fresh sardines. I just took note of it because it reminded me of when I was in Portugal in the seventies. There was a carnival in town, and there were pots of boiling octopus on almost every street corner. In my mind, seeing all that fish was a bit unusual.

Later that day when Cenk came home from work, he told us that he had something special for us for dinner. When we were in town, we passed some bakeries, and I was certain one of the lovely pastries or beautifully decorated cakes was the surprise. I was so excited that I could hardly wait. To my dismay, the surprise was not a sweet treat at all; we were going to have fried sardines for supper. I attempted to look excited, or at least interested. And, because we walked a lot that day, and it was hours since lunch, we were all hungry. I have to admit that the fried sardines were really quite tasty. Gerrit was very adventuresome and tried every type of food that was served during our stay, as did I, more out of politeness than anything. But, Hanneke just couldn't. She subsisted on the fresh bread and tangerine juice we were served at every meal. So, all in all, we were all satisfied. My children have grown up to be very adventuresome regarding foods from all cultures, having lived in foreign countries for extended periods of time.

On the last day, we were in Kusadasi, we took a bus to Ephesus and walked in the footsteps of St. Paul. After we were there a short time, the kids got thirsty and we set out looking for a pop machine. Amazingly, we found one, and all was well for the next little while. It was incredible just being in Ephesus, such an important city in Biblical times. We visited the small dwelling where Jesus's mother Mary lived with John, the disciple Jesus entrusted her with. We were told by our guide that Mother Mary lived in this place and that she eventually died there. Catholics believe that Mary did not actually die, but that she was taken to Heaven alive, or "Assumed." I am Catholic, and I believe in the Assumption. I converted to Catholicism since my trip to Turkey, not because of my experience, but I do think it influenced how I interpret my belief. My time in Ephesus continues to impact my life today.

My final memory of Turkey is of our flight back to Saudi Arabia. Prior to even getting on the Turkish Airlines flight to Riyadh, it became obvious that the flight was going to be filled with pilgrims on their way to Mecca for Hajj. Our flight would be stopping in Jeddah, and those on Pilgrimage would deplane there. When we finally boarded the plane, it was evident that we were the only Americans on the plane, for that matter, the only travelers not making a pilgrimage to Mecca. As we took our seats and began to get settled, It appeared to be the first time many had ever been on an airplane because they didn't know what to do. I remember an older woman who was seated in front of us, smiling from cheek to cheek, holding up the life preserver she had taken from under her seat. She seemed to want to give it to me, or she just wanted to show it to me, I wasn't sure. I could not understand her, so I just smiled. We all just smiled at each other.

When it came time for prayer, everyone went into the bathrooms one by one to wash their hands and feet. I found out the hard way when I walked into the bathroom wearing the airplane socks I was issued prior to take-off. So, when my kids and I needed to use the bathroom, I needed to wipe the sinks and tidy the area before we used it. I did that a lot during the flight that day. It was a most interesting experience. And, the company was very friendly and pleasant. I've said this about so many of my life experiences, but truly, "Who does this kind of thing?" I'm not certain my kids even registered that this event was really quite remarkable. I have never forgotten it.

Before I traveled to Turkey, many women warned me that I may find Turkish men very rude. My experience was quite the opposite. Perhaps, it was because I was traveling with children, I'll never know, but our drivers, those driving the taxis and buses we rode were very helpful and respectful. My friend Fatma's husband Cenk was nothing but a gentleman; he made sure that my children were comfortable in his home and that we enjoyed our time while we were in Turkey. He and Fatma made our hotel reservations, arranged for the bus trip from Istanbul to Kusadasi, and they met us at our destination. Fatma and I were good friends, but I had never met her husband or niece before. They were wonderful to us, and I have never forgotten their hospitality.

We stayed in contact for some time, but after I returned to the States, we lost contact. Life got busy and we didn't have the internet then. I lost the little address book that had all my important addresses and phone numbers, and it grieves me that to this day that I have never found it. Every now and then, I look online to see if I can locate Fatma or her husband, but I have not yet been successful.

Chapter Ten
# EGYPTIAN HOLIDAY
Work and Play

I was very fortunate to work at the hospital in Riyadh when I did, as money seemed to be readily available for education and travel for my position. Sometime after the war was over, an American trained Pediatric Cardiologist appeared on our ward one day. His focus was the care of children who required cardiac catheterizations and basic cardiac surgeries. My ward was to be designated for this new program. I took care of Pediatric Cardiology patients post-operatively when I worked in Galveston, but that was in the early eighties. The specialty had evolved since that time, and I was eager for the opportunity to learn and expand my ward's expertise. My Nursing Administrator recommended a Pediatric Cardiology Conference that was being held in Cairo later that year. She had just received the brochure in the mail and told me that she'd see to it that I have the time off and be able to go if I wanted. What an incredible opportunity! I didn't want to turn it down but had to make sure Murray and Kathy weren't planning to be gone at the same time. Thankfully, it all worked out, and I was soon on my way to Egypt!

I was pretty fearless (maybe stupid) and determined back in those days. Thinking about it now, I'm a bit surprised that I actually went to Cairo for the conference. I had decided to go to the conference sometime in the summer of 1992 and was getting pretty excited about my trip. I was really most excited about the conference because I saw it as a way to be better informed about the latest standards of care for children with heart conditions. Don't get me wrong, I was interested in visiting Egypt, but I have to admit I was travel-weary and didn't know how much sightseeing I planned to do. It was October of 1992, and the news reports that two Russian tourists had recently been murdered in Egypt. Shortly before I was scheduled to leave for Cairo, there had been another attack. I honestly barely gave the thought of canceling a second thought, I had been looking forward to this conference for months. I guess living through the Gulf Crisis, with scuds falling from the Riyadh sky while sitting in my bed, I was less affected by the threat of danger. I guess I saw it as a possibility that could happen anywhere.

Many of my friends were concerned that I was planning to travel despite the recent acts of violence against foreigners visiting Egypt. I remember saying that I would plan to travel as planned, but would be alert to the slightest roadblock for my trip to proceed, and cancel if indicated. That's how I looked at life. If I wasn't completely certain what decision was the right one, I would decide to proceed cautiously, and abandon the idea or plan if there were too many roadblocks, or if my plan was not good for all concerned.

When the time came, I boarded the plane and we landed safely, which was a great start to the trip. Nothing to stop me, at least. I do recall that there were more attacks on tour buses reported, but luckily we remained unscathed. However, one night the conference hosted an evening lecture at a heart hospital in Cairo, and quite unexpectedly a group of fundamentalists took over the lecture, shouting and demanding that the lecture conclude immediately.

Guards came in and quelled the agitators, and they were quickly ushered out. The episode was a verbal altercation only, but most of us ran for cover. We were told by our chaperones that the men were Islamic fundamentalists, unhappy that foreigners were in the country teaching high-tech medical solutions to Egyptian physicians. That didn't make sense to me back then, but I was still fairly naive about how religious extremists forced their agenda. I know now that restricting education and curbing progress is a tactic often used by dictators and those wielding control without the consent of a majority in maintaining control of a country's future. It was pretty surreal. We were ducking under the table and chairs. In my mind's eye, I can still see many of the doctors in attendance hiding under the table beside me. Even more unbelievable is the fact that when that incident was over, we continued with the lecture. Unreal!

My Egyptian experience was quite amazing. I was only there about a week, but it was life-changing as were so many of my experiences in the Middle East. I arrived on a Thursday, which is equivalent to our Saturday, and the conference was to begin Saturday morning. Since Saudi

Arabia is just across the Red Sea, I was able to leave Riyadh in the morning and arrive in Cairo by mid-afternoon. I arrived in my hotel room around 3 pm and turned on CNN. That was my favorite thing to do when I traveled while living in the Middle East. I don't think we had CNN in Saudi Arabia, and I used to love to hear James Earl Jones say "This is CNN," in his distinctive melodic voice. I found it very soothing for some reason, it reminded me of home.

After a brief nap and a shower, I went down to the hotel restaurant for a light dinner. I briefly scanned the dining room to scope out anyone that looked like they were attending the Cardiology Conference, but how would I really know. After the conference started, it became clear that there were many fellow attendees in the restaurant that first night. Because I was alone, I had two options, go back to my room and wait to resurface in the morning, or take the opportunity to do a little exploring before dark. So, after dinner, I made my way outside to see what I could see.

When I arrived outside, I noticed that many of the hotel guests were sitting on a short wall in front of the hotel. It was really quite funny, we were all just sitting there watching the cars go by. Most of the people were in groups of twos or threes, except for me, I was alone. I sat there not knowing if I should remain or go to my room. What was I waiting for, nothing was really happening. As I considered my options, I noticed a middle-aged man exiting an older model Mercedes and walking towards me. He asked me if I'd like to take a tour of Giza and the surrounding neighborhood. His request took me by surprise, but since he wore a badge identifying him as a taxi driver, I considered it. At first, I said, "I don't know, " but as I reconsidered, I quickly replied, "Yes. Thank you." I couldn't believe I said yes, and off I went in this taxi to see the sites of this ancient city most only read about in books.

We went to Giza and then visited the Pyramids at dusk. The vision of the Pyramids in person was breathtaking, made only more unbelievable by the fact that I was riding around Giza in a Mercedes taxi, alone with a driver I didn't know. As I've said before, "Who does that?" The taxi driver took very good care of me as he showed me all the sites he thought were most important during the time we had. As the sun began to set over this enchanted place, he continued to drive through the streets, highlighting historical places and facts that enriched the evening.

After the Pyramids, we were off to visit an apparently famous Flower Essence shop. The owner had shared with me how he had shared a cup of tea with movie stars and other celebrities, while they were in the region to take in the sights. His shop was well known for its exotic and rare flower essences, and for the right price, the essence master would craft a floral essence best suited to your lifestyle and personality, While I was there, he took out a photo album, and began to show me photos of those who had visited over the years, most notably Mick Jagger with one of his wives and another of the Beatles. I really can't remember whose picture I saw, it took us at least a half-hour to look at all the photos. He was a most interesting and seemingly eccentric human being. Of course, I could not leave without my own collection of flower essences, as well as the beautiful bottles needed to store them. I became a naturopathic doctor in 2000, and have learned all about the power of flower essences. When I visited the essence shop in Giza, I thought my purchases were only slightly weaker versions of perfumes. I know now that what

I was in the presence of was very magical, which better explains this gentleman's eccentric nature.

I'm not quite certain how we had time for one more stop, but we did. I was fortunate that most of the evening I was able to converse in Arabic and English with my driver, and he was able to understand me. The next stop was an art studio that featured Egyptian papyrus paintings. I purchased four paintings, The Tree of Life, Upper and Lower Egypt, a Scarab, and Horus and Nefertiti. Our individual names were written in Arabic and Hieroglyphics to personalize the picture I chose for each one of us. Today, these papyruses are prominently hung in the entryway of my home. What a beautiful reminder of such an incredible journey. The evening was magical, and thankfully, I made it back to the hotel safely. After paying the taxi driver the fee we agreed upon, I was off to bed.

Once in bed, I found it hard to sleep, for the next day I was planning to visit the famous Cairo Museum. It was said that at the time I visited, there were more artifacts and statues and treasure roped off and not available prepared for viewing than all the Egyptian items in all the museums throughout the world. I was also so excited for the conference to begin, but I have to admit that I had no idea of what to expect. I was quite fortunate to be invited to this Pediatric Cardiology conference. There were Pediatric cardiologists from all over the world and I was the only nurse in attendance. It was a great opportunity to participate in cutting-edge lectures presented by top doctors from America, Europe, Asia, and the Middle East. During my time in Cairo, I became friends with a handful of doctors and their spouses, a physician and his nurse wife from Chicago, a brilliant heart surgeon out of Stanford, and a Belgian Pediatric cardiologist and her husband who was a famous sculptor.

This experience was not only one of travel, education, and sightseeing, it was transformational, in that I shared my life with those I met. We exchanged ideas of our hopes and dreams in the conversations and experiences we shared along the way. I also became friendly with an Egyptian cardiologist from Alexandria. There had been a recent earthquake, and the city was experiencing aftershocks, so after the last day of lectures, she invited me to her condo so I won't be alone. The afternoon and evening I spent with my friend and her 20-something daughter was very eye-opening. My friend's daughter and I ventured into town for some items her mother needed for the evening. We walked through rubble, climbing over mounds of buckled concrete to get to where we were going, and then back home again. I felt like I was a time traveler. This ancient city had survived pillaging and war in the past, and parts of the city lay in ruins that day, which seemed reminiscent of the past. But, at its core, the city was resilient and remained alive and vibrant. On returning home, my friend whom I had only met a day or two previously, handled me with kid gloves, making sure I was fed and had an opportunity to rest.

I was ushered into the guest bedroom to take a nap in preparation for the Nile Dinner Cruise we would attend that evening. As I awakened from my nap, I experienced an aftershock and almost fell out of bed. We had become accustomed to the minor shocks, so we pretty much ignored them and prepared ourselves for the evening's event. Dressed in our finest, we arrived at the boat excited for the Mediterranean dinner that was planned and the entertainment to follow. As we waited to board, a young couple had just completed their wedding vows at the tail end of their wedding ceremony. As they kissed, we gave them a standing ovation. They seemed happy to receive our good wishes and soon disembarked the boat and walked away ready to start their married life together. What a lovely way to start the evening! I was surprised that the bride wore what would be considered a traditional wedding dress in the States. I guess things around the world really aren't that different after all.

Our dinner cruise returned to shore sometime before midnight, and as we docked, a young Egyptian cardiology resident, whom I recognized from the conference, offered to take us back to our hotel. Throughout the conference, this young man was very instrumental in keeping things on time and running smoothly. He apparently was from an influential family in Cairo and "had connections." Regardless, he was most helpful, always there when an interpreter was needed for the various educational events and demonstrations. As we prepared to return to the hotel, he talked us into going to an all-night cafe. I couldn't tell you what we ate, but I do know that we did not return home to our hotel rooms until very early the next morning. That would have been just fine, but we were scheduled to leave the hotel for the airport to catch the plane to Karnak at 6 am. Oh my! Thank goodness I was much younger then. I'm getting tired just thinking about it.

We all gathered our bags and off to the airport we went. We were scheduled to tour Upper Egypt and visit the historical sites in the region. The following three days were some of the most enjoyable of my life. I was with others I had met at the conference, the couple from Belgium, as well as the doctor and his wife from Chicago and the Stanford surgeon. After spending the day in Karnak and visiting the Valley of the Kings that first day, we boarded a small cruise ship and set off up the Nile. Our tour guide met us in Karnak, and he remained at our side until we returned to Cairo days later. He was a very talented and charming young man who had studied Egyptology at Oxford. He was somewhat worldly, and informed us in a way that only a native to Egypt could, proud of his heritage, yet educated in the history of the region at a more complex level.

We set off on the water at dusk that first night. The sky was a muted blue, and off in the distance, a donkey and his master made their way on the banks of the River Nile.

The scene reminded me of one I imagined when reading stories based around the time of Moses. The boat leisurely sailed upriver, with our trip culminating in Lake Nasser and the historic Abu Simbel. Our guide joined us for meals, as we remained long after we finished eating, sharing stories of our varied life experiences. I truly have never laughed so hard in my whole life, my rib cage and abdominal muscles were so sore as if I had overdone it in the gym. The evenings offered entertainment, and one night there was an Egyptian dance contest. I was familiar with the dance format because of all the dancing we did at our girl parties, so I had the courage to participate, and even won a prize. All those girl parties paid off. The cruise was so much fun and I was able to enjoy authentic Egyptian Middle Eastern cuisine. Every country has its own flair and unless you are in the actual country, various ethnic foods take on the flavor of the host country. We went to shore from time to time, but the grand finale was our visit to Aswan and the temples of Abu Simbel. We took in the sites of Aswan as we sailed the calm waters of Lake Nasser one morning and visited Abu Simbel after lunch. The experience was breathtaking and virtually indescribable.

We were told that the monuments needed to be moved in an effort to avoid flooding that was expected to occur as a result of the River Nile being dammed. An international team of engineers began the process of relocating the Abu Simbel Temple in 1963 and it was completed in 1968. It is said that the project cost $40 million at the time, which was thought to be well worth it, as it is considered the world's biggest monument. Just telling this story makes me so grateful to have been in its presence.

The entire trip was one I could not have anticipated. I was truly left in awe after experiencing the combination of ancient and modern-day Egypt and spending time at the feet of the world's most magnificent monuments. I was a fairly experienced traveler, so I had expectations of my visit being interesting and adventurous, but what I received was so much more. To walk in the footsteps of Mark Anthony, Alexander the Great and Cleopatra, as we visited the Sphinx was so inspiring. It was incredible to think that at some point, my path may have crossed where Mary, Joseph, and Jesus passed when they were refugees.

I was so fortunate to experience Egyptian hospitality during my stay, as I spent hours with my new friends drinking tea, and in conversation and laughter. We had time to talk about our families, and what we hoped to accomplish in our careers. I truly believe that during these moments in time, through the exchange of ideas, without an agenda or bias, I had a wonderful opportunity to see the world at large, one person at a time.

## Chapter Eleven
# A Homestay in Morocco
### Visiting My Daughter

My daughter joined the Peace Corps after college and accepted an assignment in Morocco. We shared a love for our time in the Middle East, which seemed to fuel her desire to be placed in an Arabic-speaking country. I was very supportive of her overseas volunteer interest and was eager for her to, perhaps, have some of the same experiences I had in my twenties.

My work as a volunteer was as a nurse in the hospital for which I had been trained and had many years of experience. Hanneke's position, on the other hand, was as a Health Worker to evaluate health and wellness gaps and develop programs to address the community's needs. She lived in a remote city in the southwestern part of Morocco, where she eventually had her own apartment. Several of her Peace Corps friends lived in nearby towns, so she wasn't completely alone. Following orientation, Hanneke lived with a host family for several weeks, as she became familiar with the region and learned about its culture, customs, and language. She was fortunate to be placed in a very welcoming and loving home, and for that, I will always be so very grateful. From all accounts, the mother and father were very protective of her began her work in their community. There were young children in the home, and Hanneke spoke of them as if she really was the big sister.

Electronic communications were not as sophisticated back in 2008, when she left home, as they are now. It was quite costly to call initially, but over time, the long-distance fees lessened and it was easier and easier to communicate by phone. We spent long conversations as she shared stories of a place I had never been, but I could relate at some level. I remember Hanneke telling me about her first Ramadan in Morocco and Eid al-Fitr, the festival that follows. I believe she was still living with her host family, and the time came to slaughter the sheep for the feast. It was customary for the whole family to witness the slaughter and participate in its blessing. It was a difficult event to witness, I know, but in being there, she demonstrated that she considered herself a part of the family.

In May of 2009, I was extremely fortunate to visit Hanneke in Morocco, and what a memorable trip it was. I landed in Casablanca and spent a day milling about like a local. Hanneke had been in Morocco for over a year, so knew the spots that were not generally frequented by tourists. After a day's respite, we were off to the train station to purchase tickets to Marrakech. We had a slight wait but arrived early so that we were certain to make the train that afternoon. The train ride to Marrakech was breathtaking, as we winded around hills and valleys of the Moroccan countryside. Once we arrived in Marrakech, we freshened up and later spent hours meandering through the open market and later dined on traditional Moroccan cuisine. It's a bit surreal to have visited both Marrakech and Casablanca, cities with such historic and nostalgic meaning.

On my third day in Morocco, we boarded the bus to Agadir, the city nearest to where Hanneke lived. If you've ever traveled by bus for a long distance in any country, it's a treat. There's usually head bobbing, falling asleep with your mouth open, and trying to figure out when is a good time to use the restroom. The bus usually makes a stop for a potty break and a bite to eat somewhere along the way, but if it's your first time on a bus, there's no telling when that might happen. To say the least, we did arrive in one piece, and since no one knew me, it didn't really matter if my mouth was wide open, or my head bobbing along the way. The important thing is that the ride was comfortable, and we arrived safely. Then, we hacked a taxi to Tiznit, our final destination.

During my time in Tiznit, I met Hanneke's host family and some of her Peace Corps friends. One day we were in town, and we ran into Hanneke's host father, and he smiled from ear to ear when he was speaking of her. It was truly heartwarming. One afternoon we were invited for tea in her host family's home. After a period of introductions and explanations of who was who, we went outside as the host mother and her sister tended the sheep as they grazed near their home. I recall Hanneke telling me that the sheep would run through the house up the stairs to the roof, which was where they stayed at night. They truly were a part of the family. We remained outside for at least an hour, perched up against the house, watching the sheep. It was very peaceful, like a form of meditation. Few words were spoken during these silent moments of wonder and watch.

I was also fortunate to meet Hanneke's colleague in her community health work. She was from Morocco, and they seemed to have a nice rapport and were very committed to the work they had started. They developed and rolled out a program in the classroom to teach children the importance of oral hygiene. The students were given toothbrushes and toothpaste and taught how to use them. In many parts of the world oral hygiene is compromised by the abundance of candy and snack food readily available. Learning the importance of oral hygiene is such an important aspect far too often ignored. It was fun collecting toothbrushes and toothpaste back home for the program. Those were fun visits.

It so happened that my last day in Tiznit coincided with the Friday Women's Cooperative Bazaar. The local women were provided encouragement and some financial backing through education and training to produce a sustainable product to market. As a result, they developed a process for pressing and bottling Moroccan Argon oil. Their target market at this time was primarily tourists, but the ability to export their product was definitely of interest to them. The day we visited the Women's Cooperative, many of the women brought crafts and bakery items for sale. I went home with many of the items, and the Moroccan Argon oil, of course. This was a fun and rewarding day, as I was able to speak to many of the women and feel a part of their world, if only for a day.

My visit was very short but jam-packed, and by the time I returned to Casablanca, I felt I had experienced a fraction of my daughter's world while living in Morocco. I was grateful for this time with her and so excited to have experienced her world and meet those with whom she spent all those many months since leaving home. It was fun to use what limited Arabic I could remember whenever an individual spoke Arabic instead of the local Berber dialect spoken in and around Tiznit.

When it came time for me to make my way back to Casablanca, we decided to take a taxi to Marrakech, hoping it would be more comfortable than riding the bus. So, we arrived at the taxi stand in Agadir in plenty of time to arrange for a ride to catch the train in plenty of time to reach the airport for my flight home. Hanneke reserved a taxi and paid for three seats in the back so we would have additional room for the journey. I can't remember how long the car ride was, but it was a bit of a journey. It so happened that the driver took on two other passengers, which was unexpected. The taxi usually seated one passenger in the front seat and three in the rear. But, we had purchased an additional seat in the back. The men were real gentlemen, and allowed us the room we had purchased, and sat upfront. At some point during the trip, I think we invited one of the men to sit in the back, as the front was quite cramped, and we felt bad seeing their cramped quarters.

As we made our way through the countryside, we climbed one hill after another. As we began up a particularly steep hill, our taxi unceremoniously overheated, and the driver needed to attend to it. It appeared that the driver was prepared for this occurrence, having a couple of jugs of water handy in the trunk. So, he filled the radiator with water, and we were off again. Just about the time we got back on the road, a bus traveling down the hill appeared to lean too far to the left and tipped over. People immediately ran to their aid, but we continued up the hill. I prayed they were all okay and felt bad that we kept going without knowing if everyone was okay. Apparently, this was a bus route my daughter routinely took when traveling home from Marrakech. According to reports, the bus was packed heavily to one side, but thankfully, no one was injured badly. It seems that following accidents of any kind, safety measures are more thoroughly enforced after the fact, which provided me some comfort in regards to Hanneke.

As I boarded my plane in Casablanca for home, my Moroccan Holiday was soon a mere memory. It is in telling the story now that I remember the many sites, smells and sounds that were so vibrant and wonderful. My time in Morocco reinforced my love for the spoken Arabic language and the many customs similar to those I experienced when living amongst the Bedouin in Saudi Arabia. My daughter was a wonderful hostess, making sure I was comfortable and had an enjoyable time. The nine days were magical and I am grateful to have revisited the time as I write about it and share it with you.

Chapter Twelve
# When An Expat Returns Home
Summer 1994

Whoever coined the phrase "You can never go home again" must have been an ExPat. Returning home after living in a country whose culture and customs are completely different is quite a shock to your system. I would often find myself thinking of an instance when I was in Riyadh, and it all seemed like a dream. It was just so hard to relate the experience to that of my life back in the States. As soon as I stepped off the plane in Phoenix, it was truly like turning a page in the book of my life. Luckily, I had a renter in my home for the four years I was away, and it was ready for me to move into on my return. During those years, I made frequent trips "home" to Phoenix and remained connected to my friends and my church. So, in all actuality, the transition was fairly smooth, except for the hole that was created by my leaving Saudi Arabia. But, that was the choice I made, for what I thought were the right reasons, and I was determined to make a good life for my children and me.

I became entrenched in my children's activities, which was a real blessing. School programs and after-school sports filled the hours of the day, and soon it was like we had lived here forever. I was fortunate that Gerrit and Hanneke went to an international school, where the class sizes were smaller than the norm, which seemed to make their transition manageable. Being in a school where there were students from other parts of the world was familiar to them, and it made me feel more comfortable, too. I worked part-time for a Pediatric Homecare company, taking care of children on ventilators. I had developed a Pediatric Ventilator training program for my nursing staff in Riyadh so we could care for a little girl who needed to be on a ventilator and couldn't be cared for in her home. As a result of my training staff and observing their skillset, I felt comfortable pursuing this specialty as a private duty nurse in the home. In a way, taking care of children who required ventilator assistance allowed me to feel connected to my staff back in Riyadh.

The years have gone by, and it's nearly thirty years since I left Saudi Arabia for the last time. I was certain I would return some day, but it was not meant to be. Life has a way of dictating how things go, sometimes no matter how hard you try to exert pressure on a desired outcome. I left nursing for a while and received my Doctorate in Naturopathic Medicine in 2000. After my kids left home and were both out of the country, I decided to revisit the possibility of working in Saudi Arabia again. As with most Travel Nursing positions, a requirement for employment is two years of current experience in the acute care setting. I began working at Phoenix Children's Hospital on the Telemetry and Airway Unit in 2007 and was determined to acquire the experience needed to return to work in the Middle East.

As fate would have it, I reconnected with someone I knew when I was in college, and we married in 2009. A return to the Middle East was no longer in the cards. Today I couldn't return if I wanted to because I'm too old. Saudi Arabia and the United Arab Emirates have an age limit for employment, and I have exceeded it, So, I believe things turned out the way they were meant to be, and I'm okay with it. Life has been good to me, and I am very grateful for the experiences I have had. I especially enjoy being able to incorporate what I learned from my experience in the Middle East into my everyday life.

A couple of years ago, I was visiting a gentleman in my capacity as a Home Health Nurse. He and his wife were from Iran, and they told me that they had lived in the United States for most of their adult lives. We readily struck up a conversation, and as the visit evolved, a big smile appeared on my patient's face. He asked me how I knew how to pronounce his name, saying that nurses usually mispronounced his name. I explained that I had lived in the Middle East many years ago, and was quite familiar with Middle Eastern names and their pronunciation.

Initially, my patient was very quiet and subdued, and by his own admission a bit anxious, as he had had many visiting nurses and generally little conversation. It seemed that the simple act of showing interest in him on a personal level eased his anxiety and allowed for my visit to be so much more comfortable for him. He proceeded to tell about growing up in Iran, and of his life in the United States. The simple act of kindness, in my smile or the greeting of Salam Alaikum, made an instant connection and familiarity when there was none when I arrived. My patient was in the twilight of his years, and in poor health. I was happy to provide some solace and enjoyment during my visit that day.

I recently watched a program on Nova that investigated how people learn to form biases. The show examined how children as young as three years old discriminated against others relative to the color of shirt they were wearing or an item that was similar or different than theirs. It was an eye-opening exercise to observe. It was determined that much of the difficulty develops when children, at a very young age, are addressed only when there is a problem. It was further noted, that in order to promote inclusiveness, it is necessary to reinforce cooperation and unity early in life. So, whether children have different colored shirts or hair or skin, when addressed in a generally positive manner, they will identify as members of a cohesive group and not look to differentiate themselves. The study found that if children are provided encouragement for cooperation, and not only addressed when there is a problem, they do not readily look for someone else to blame besides themselves. So, accentuating the good each child does throughout the day results in the group feeling better about themselves. No one wants to be accused of wrongdoing, but it's often easier to pin the blame on the one who looks different.

As a part of the series, there was a story about a project developed to determine whether it was possible to integrate Arabic and Israeli soccer players because of their unified love of the sport. The documentary "Sons of Sakhalin United" followed the B'nei Sakhnin soccer team throughout the 2004-2005 season. The team was formed as an experiment in co-existence between Arab Israelis, Jews, and foreigners, as they competed together under a Jewish coach. In the beginning, one Israeli player's family questioned whether their son would be safe in the Arab town in which the team was based, and at times, vindictive fans called out ethnic slurs during the games. Over time, the success of the team won over fans and soccer players alike. One team member later stated that he "no longer views his teammates through the lens of their et[hnicity]. And the citizens of the small Arab-Israeli town "e[mbrace] the Jewish coach as their own." If peace is possible in the playing of a mutually loved sport by those who would normally hate each other, then perhaps peace is possible in the world at large.

I run into people from time to time who have lived in Saudi Arabia, and we often share similar experiences of the friendships we cherished. My hope is that I am able to shine a light on the lives of real people, individuals making it through life day to day like myself and many of my family and friends. I am heartened by a story my husband shares about the owner of a tire shop he routinely visits. It seems that over time, he and the owner expanded their topic of conversation from cars to life in general. The shop owner told my husband of home country Somalia, and that he was Muslim, sharing some of what that entailed. One Ramadan, he explained the need for fasting and how the entire family gathered together to break the fast at sundown throughout the entire Holy month. He even sent pictures to my husband's phone one evening to document the event. It seemed the two men enjoyed the fact that they could relate to each other regardless of their obvious differences. My husband has a new story every time he returns home from that shop.

The world is such a different place today than it was when I left Saudi Arabia in 1994. Many might say it's better because Saddam Hussain and Osama Bin Laden are dead, but unfortunately, there remains much evil in the world. The government of Saudi Arabia has been in the news far too often for involvement in unspeakable crimes, and crises loom on the horizon in many of the countries in the Middle East. However, we don't have to look further than our own country to find discord and hate crimes, which saddens my heart. I personally have some strongly held beliefs, some very different than some family and friends. I choose not to discuss our differing opinions but know that that really isn't the solution.

In the end, it seems that love truly is the answer. Most religions have at their core love for one another. Jesus told his disciples in Matthew 22:39 that "You shall love your neighbor as yourself." From my perspective, this is far easier said than done. I have searched for the secret to carry out this commandment for much of my life. More recently, I have followed many of the teachings of Deepak Chopra, and I love what he recommends if you are challenged in seeing another's point of view or have a fractured relationship. My understanding is that it is possible to heal relationships and find common ground with those you disagree through love.

So, I can't get along with someone by purposely avoiding conflict or thinking of the right thing to say. But, through silent meditation, while asking what is best for all concerned without judgement, I can find a way to get along others, starting at home. If I can get along at home, and accept my husband and other family members for who they are, I have a chance to expand that to the world at large. And perhaps, one person at a time, the world can be a better place for you and me.

## Chapter Thirteen
# SENDING SONG

This is My Song by Jean Sibelius (1865-1957)

This is my song, oh God of all the nations,
a song of peace for lands afar and mine.
This is my home, the country where my heart is;
here are my hopes, my dreams, my holy shrine;
but other hearts in other lands are beating
with hopes and dreams as true and high as mine.
My country's skies are bluer than the ocean,
and sunlight beams on clover leaf and pine.
But other lands have sunlight too and clover,
and skies are everywhere as blue as mine.
This is my song, oh God of all the nations;
a song of peace for their land and for mine.

This is My Song was composed by Jean Sibelius (1865-1957). A song of hope that expresses the love of nation and an end to that which divides us from others.

# Appendix
## The Five Pillars of Islam

1. A Muslim believes in the One God (Allah) and of the Prophethood of Muhammad. Belief in the One God, Allah, and reverence for the Prophet Muhammad. "There is none worthy of worship except God (Allah) and Muhammad (Peace Be Upon Him) is the messenger of God."

2. To establish the practice of praying five times a day. A believer of Islam is to pray five times a day. Although it is preferable to worship together in a mosque, a Muslim made pray almost anywhere.

3. Concern for and almsgiving giving to the needy. Charity and Concern for the needy are required of a believer of Islam. An important principle of Islam is that everything belongs to God, and that wealth is therefore

held by human beings in trust. It is believed that possessions are purified by setting aside a portion for those in need and for the society in general.

4. Muslims purify themselves through fasting in the month of Ramadan. Observance of Fasting during the month of Ramadan is required of a believer. Every year, Muslims fast from dawn until sundown during Ramadan: abstaining from food, drink, and sexual relations with their spouses. Those who are sick, elderly, or on a journey, as well as women who are menstruating, pregnant or nursing, are permitted to break the fast and make up an equal number of days later in the year if they are healthy and able. Children begin to fast at puberty.

5. A pilgrimage to Mecca is expected of those who are able. Muslims make a Pilgrimage to Mecca once in a lifetime if physically and financially able. The annual Hajj begins in the 12th month of the Islamic lunar year. Pilgrims wear simple garments that strip away any distinction of class and culture so that all stand equal before God.

# REFERENCES

1. A Chronology: The House of Saudi Frontline, www.pbs.org, updated Aug 1, 2005.

2. Bedouin, New World Encyclopedia contributors, New World Encyclopedia, 13 December 2016, Page Version ID: 1001935.

3. Building a New Middle East through Soccer and Weight Loss, Juliet Lapidos, The Forward, May 18, 2007.

4. Ryan's Adventure Learning the Five Pillars of Islam, The Sincere Seeker, Amazon Books, June 22, 2021.

5. The Kingdom: Arabia and the House of Sa'ud, Robert Lacy, Hardcourt Brace Jovanovich, Inc 1982.